MUFFIN, DIGBY AND PETAL

FAMILY OF RESCUE DOGS BOOK 7

BRIAN L PORTER

This seventh book in my Family of Rescue Dogs series, is dedicated to the memory of Sasha, who's story was the first in the series, and who sadly crossed the Rainbow Bridge in the summer of 2020, and also to the memory of Dexter, our beautiful 'bird-dog' who gained his wings one year before Sasha. Both are still much loved, sadly missed and they both definitely left their paw prints on my heart.

Sasha and Dexter, now together forever

Petal, Muffin and Digby on their 4th birthday

INTRODUCTION

Welcome to Book 7 of my Family of Rescue Dogs series. Readers of previous books in the series, all of which have featured the stories of individual dogs, might be wondering why this seventh book in the series contains the life stories of not one, but three dogs. The answer is really quite simple. The three dogs featured in the following pages are two sisters, Muffin and Petal, and their brother Digby, all the product of one litter of pups.

How we came to adopt three puppies from one litter will be explained at the beginning of the book and as their story progresses, I'm sure you'll realise why it would have been simply impossible to separate their stories into three individual books and why it made logical sense to combine their three stories into this one, longer than usual volume.

While I have your attention, (at least I hope I have), I'd like to take this opportunity to say a massive thank you to all my loyal readers who voted for *Remembering Dexter* in the two most recent book awards. Thanks to your support, the book, which was written in tribute to the life of Dexter, who passed away after a long illness, not only quickly became a #1 best-seller in the UK and the USA, but went on to win, first of all, The Best Indie Book of the Year, 2019, as voted for by the subscribers to Readfree.ly, from over two thousand entries, and then was the winner of the Best Nonfiction Book of 2019 award in the Critters.org (formerly Preditors & Editors) Annual Readers Poll. The book then became a three-time award-winner by winning the Best Non-Fiction Category in the 2020 Reader Choice Book Awards. Dexter had quite a following on Facebook, and I received many messages of love and condolence when he died in June 2019. Thank you to you all, your love and support was greatly appreciated.

Remembering Dexter

1

2012, NOT A VINTAGE YEAR

HOW OFTEN IN our lives do we find something good coming from something tragic or unpleasant? 2012 was just such a year for us, especially for my dear wife, Juliet. It began well enough, when she saw an advertisement in the local newspaper offering Staffy puppies for sale. I'd promised her that if she found a suitable puppy, we could add one to our family of rescue dogs, so having seen the advert she drew my attention to it, and I made a telephone call and we arranged to go and see the puppies for sale.

Of course, it's not too difficult to fall in love when faced with a litter of beautiful little puppies, and Juliet, (and me of course), were no different from anyone else. Having seen the pups, and played with them in the owner's garden, it quickly became a matter of choosing which one we would take. Although I fell for a little one that was black with white feet and chest, this was to be Juliet's puppy, so I left the decision to her. She eventually chose a tiny, brindle coloured pup, and after the required cost of the little dog was handed over, we went home with the latest member of our 'doggie family'.

Chudleigh

I can't really recall how we came up with a name for Juliet's new 'baby' but eventually we settled on 'Chudleigh'. The puppy soon settled into our home and family and in no time at all he became 'Juliet's baby'. He followed her everywhere and was like her second shadow. He was a fast learner and was soon house trained and loved going for walks with his new human 'Mummy'.

Sadly, our time with little Chudleigh was all too brief, as at the age of eight months, we were to lose our little boy in particularly harrowing circumstances, which I won't put in print, as the loss of her baby boy was to have a devastating effect on Juliet. Even now, seven years later, she finds it impossible to get rid of the T-shirt I had made for her with his picture on the front and printed with 'Chudleigh's Mum', and she still sheds a tear from time to time, at the memory of that gorgeous little boy. (I've still got his name tag in a box, too).

All I knew at that time was my dear wife fell into what could only be described as a time of deep depression. Although we still had the rest of 'pack' to love and care for, I'd often find her tearful and sad, and it didn't take a brain surgeon to work out that the loss of her special puppy had totally devastated her.

Juliet with Chudleigh

Weeks passed and my poor Juliet seemed to be slipping further and further into a morass of depression. Wherever she went, whatever she did, she couldn't get poor Chudleigh out of her mind. Even a visit to the doctor, which I virtually pleaded with her to attend, did little to help, despite him prescribing anti-depressants to help her.

Knowing what was causing her depressed state of mind, I decided that there was only one thing that might help her become more like herself once again.

"You need a new puppy," I said to her one day, completely out of the blue.

"What for?" she asked.

"Because unless you have a puppy for you to give your love to, you're never going to get over losing Chudleigh. A new puppy isn't a replacement, you can never replace him, I know that, but you will have a new pup to focus on and that way you won't be thinking about him all the time."

"I'll think about it," she replied, and I left it at that. I didn't want to push her into it. When and if it happened, it had to be Juliet's own choice, her decision.

It was four or five weeks later before anything was said about my offer of a new puppy. I'd noticed that Juliet had been buying our local newspaper more frequently than usual, and I'd thought she may be looking at adverts for puppies for sale. On this occasion she confirmed my suspicions.

"There's some puppies for sale in the paper," she said one day as I walked into the house with two dogs after we'd been for our afternoon walk.

"Really?" I said, trying to sound both innocent and surprised at the same time.

"Yes," she replied, sounding brighter than she had in a long time. "It says here there's a litter of five puppies for sale, staffy/springer crosses, fifty pounds each."

I could sense a new enthusiasm in her voice, and I commented,

"Staffy/springers? I bet they're unusual looking pups."

"Please, can we phone up and find out about them?"

"Of course," I responded. "Pass me the paper."

She did so and I saw she'd drawn a big ring round the advert.

I picked up my phone and dialled the number given in the advert. The lady who replied sounded very nice, gave us the address and said, if we were interested, we could call anytime to see the pups. Knowing how much this could mean to Juliet, I told her we'd be there in ten minutes, as the address she'd given wasn't far away from our home, and was located very near the town's racecourse, and would be easy to find.

Juliet's excitement was palpable as we drove towards the puppies' location. As we pulled up on the street close to the address, she was out of car almost as soon as I turned the ignition off.

We were greeted at the door by the lady I'd spoken to on the phone and after introducing ourselves she led us into the lounge, where her husband sat, with two dogs at his feet. These turned out to be the parents of the pups. The mother was a beautiful white and black Staffordshire bull terrier, and the father was a very handsome-looking red and white springer spaniel. Both dogs were calm and extremely gentle as they both greeted us with licks and allowed us to stroke and pet them. We saw that as a good sign. If the puppies had inherited their parents' friendly natures, they should make excellent family pets.

"Well, I suppose you'd better come and see the puppies," the lady, whose name was Jane, told us, after we'd spent a few minutes interacting with the adult dogs. Jane led us through to the kitchen, where there, in a large dog bed in one corner, the five puppies were located. That is, they were until they saw Jane and us, and suddenly we were surrounded by five little balls of fur, full of excitement, their little tails wagging furiously and a couple of them making little puppy noises. Jane's husband, John, joined us at that point and the four of us spent the next few minutes picking up and fussing the five tiny pups.

"They're all gorgeous," Juliet said, with a big smile on her face as she stroked one of the pups as she held it in her arms.

"They certainly are," I agreed.

"I have to tell you," Jane then pointed out one of the pups, a black and white one with striking markings, "this one is reserved for our son. He saw them and instantly asked if he could have it, because of its markings."

"And this one," her husband said as he picked up the smallest puppy, "is staying with us. He's a little runt and we don't feel it would be right to sell him in case his owners don't give him the extra care and attention he'll need. You're welcome to choose from the other three."

By reducing our choice from five to three options, you could be forgiven for thinking this made our task easier, but no, the more we interacted with the three remaining puppies, the harder the decision became. They were all so lovable, cute and cuddly. I personally liked a little black and white girl puppy, with very pretty markings, like the petals on a flower, while Juliet was leaning more towards another puppy, smaller than my choice, black with a white chest. The one remaining pup was a little boy with an attractive brindle coat covering most of his body, but with a white head and chest and a patch over one eye.

"Well, my darling, which one is it going to be?" I asked, and Juliet finally decided on the little black one, who she was cuddling in her arms as she spoke.

"I'd like this one, please," she replied, and I nodded in agreement.

The choice made, I took out my wallet and handed over the

fifty pounds to Jane, who in turn passed the cash to her husband who put it safely in his pocket.

"We need to go and get a few things for her before we can take her, new bed, collar and lead and so on, so if it's ok with you, I'll call tomorrow morning to pick her up."

"That'll be perfectly okay," John responded, and with our business done, his wife offered to make tea or coffee for us.

"Coffee for me please," I said, while Juliet opted for tea.

We spent a convivial half hour chatting with the couple, while the puppies were placed back in their bed in the kitchen. We explained to Jane and John about our family of rescued dogs, and they seemed impressed with our love and devotion to our animals. They also told us how their own dogs had managed to 'come together' accidentally and the puppies hadn't been planned, but they were happy that when they arrived, they were all fit and healthy and were pleased that the little black one now seemed to have found a perfect home. Jane then asked Juliet if she had any ideas on what she was going to name the puppy and Juliet instantly replied,

"I want to call her Muffin."

"That's a lovely name," Jane exclaimed, obviously loving the name.

"Yes, it's unusual too," was my response. "Okay, Muffin it is."

Juliet was delighted and after we'd said our goodbyes, for now, to the couple, we immediately drove into town to buy everything we'd need in order to be ready for Muffin's arrival the following day.

There was a large pet store close to the market in the centre of town, and after finding a space in the nearby car park, we soon found all we needed in the store, and happily set off for home. Later that day, when our girls arrived home from school, we told them about the puppy, and they were both delighted and excited at the prospect of new puppy arriving the next day. They'd had no idea we were even thinking about getting a puppy. Juliet's depression had been kept from them as far as was possible, although they knew their mum was still unhappy about losing little Chudleigh.

Later that evening, as we were relaxing in the lounge, and the girls were in bed, Juliet suddenly said,

"Are you sure I've made the right choice?"

"What do you mean?" I asked her.

"The puppy," she said. "I know you preferred the little black and white one. I'm not sure now."

"Don't be silly," I smiled and sat beside her with my arm round her shoulder. "This is supposed to be your puppy, and I left the choice entirely up to you. I'm sure little Muffin will be a perfect addition to our family. Stop worrying about whether or not you made the right choice. Of course you did."

"It's just that they were all so gorgeous. I'd have liked to bring them all home with us."

I squeezed her hand, reassuringly.

"I know you would have," I said, "but you've made a choice and we'll stick with it. Just look forward to tomorrow and your new puppy."

"I really do wish we could have taken them all," she replied. "But I know that's not possible."

"I wish we could too, but we can't afford to buy an endless stream of puppies," I said, as an idea began to form in my mind. The idea grew stronger in my mind overnight and in the morning, when Juliet went up for her bath after we'd fed the dogs, I quietly picked up my mobile phone, went to the back door where she couldn't hear me from upstairs and made a 'secret' phone call to John and Jane's number.

Jane answered her phone on the second ring, and I explained, quietly, the reason for my call.

"Good morning, Jane. It's Brian, calling about the dog. Don't worry, we haven't changed our minds or anything, in fact, quite the opposite. I want to surprise Juliet and I'm hoping that since yesterday, you haven't sold the little black and white one I liked."

"No, we haven't. Do you want to take that one instead?" she asked.

"Oh no, not at all. I'd like to take the little black and white one as well as the black one Juliet picked. She was wittering all evening, wondering if she'd chosen the right puppy. This way, the problem is solved to everyone's satisfaction."

Jane laughed and agreed that I could have the black and white puppy as well. I quickly ended the call, just in time as it happened, as Juliet came down the stairs a couple of minutes later.

"Were you on the phone just now? I thought I heard you talking to someone when I came out of the bathroom."

"Yes," I replied, thinking on my feet to come up with a believable response. Keeping as close to the truth as possible, I explained that I'd called Jane to confirm that I'd be calling for Muffin at around ten a.m. and wanted to make sure that time was still okay with her and John.

"Oh, right. That was a good idea," Juliet agreed, and inwardly, I breathed a sigh of relief. I'd got away with it and my secret was safe. The time flew that morning. We walked our dogs as normal and before we knew it, the time had come for me to drive the few miles to collect what Juliet believed was the one puppy, little Muffin.

When I arrived at the home of John and Jane, they welcomed me as if I was an old friend and insisted I had a cup of coffee with them before leaving with the two puppies, who they had in the lounge, ready and waiting for me on my arrival. I didn't mind staying for coffee as it gave me a little time to play with the two puppies before taking them away from the only home they'd known up to this point in their lives. I handed over the money to pay for the second puppy and when I was ready to leave, Jane carried the two puppies to the car for me, and gently placed them in the bed that Juliet had placed in the rear of our Ford Mondeo estate car to make it a nice, comfortable and cosy means of transporting the puppy, (remember she was only expecting one).

As I pulled away from John and Jane's home, the couple stood on the pavement outside their front gate and waved me and the puppies off. As I reached the end of the street, I gave them a quick toot on the horn to say goodbye and was quickly on the road to home. I couldn't wait to see Juliet's face when I turned up with not one, but two new puppies to add to our doggy family.

2

MUFFIN, PETAL AND A SURROGATE MUM

THE TWO PUPPIES were extremely well-behaved on the journey to their new home. Although they were too tiny to climb up and look out of the car windows, they made no sound at all, so they weren't whining or showing any signs of distress as far as I could ascertain. When I pulled up outside our house I quickly exited the car and went to the rear to lift the tailgate to see how they were. As I reached the back of the car, Juliet came out of the house and made her way towards me, anxious and excited to see her new puppy, her little Muffin. As she drew near, I took a step backwards to give her a clear view into the rear luggage compartment.

A few seconds later, her face was an absolute picture as she took in the sight of the two tiny tail-wagging puppies in the bed in the back of the car.

"There's two!" she exclaimed, looking at me as if to ask me how and why one had become two.

"That's right," I said grinning from ear to ear. "You said you weren't sure last night, so I called Jane this morning and arranged to get them both."

"You sneaky sod!" she laughed. "That's what you were talking about on the phone this morning. That was so thoughtful of you. Thank you, my darling," and she gave me a big kiss.

"That's alright," I replied. "Now are you going to stand here all morning, or shall we get our new babies into the house?"

"Of course," Juliet was so excited, as she picked up the two puppies, who were both wagging their tails and quickly smothered her face in little doggy kisses as she held them close to her face, kissing them in return. "And we need to think of a name for this little one," she indicated the black and white puppy.

"I think I have a name," I said, as we walked down the garden path towards the gate to our back garden. "Look at her markings. They're like flower petals, so I thought we could call her Petal."

"That's unusual," Juliet replied. "I like it, and anyway, as I named Muffin it's only fair you should name the second pup. Petal it is, then."

We then followed our usual routine, which had proved successful in the past. Juliet handed the two pups over to me and she went indoors to get ready to allow our dogs to meet them. I carried them into the back garden, where I gently placed them on the ground and gave them a few minutes to explore their new surroundings before allowing the rest of our dogs to meet them. The puppies loved the open space they discovered in our quite large back garden. In typical puppy fashion they ran around, stopping and sniffing at all the different scents they encountered, which of course, included the scents of all our dogs. Then, they decided on a spot of puppy play, jumping up and down and climbing on each other, until I decided the time was right for them to meet 'the pack'.

Juliet had been watching us through the window and was

waiting for me to give her the thumbs-up signal which would tell her to allow a couple of the dogs out, as we wouldn't want to overwhelm the puppies by allowing them all to come out at once and overpower or frighten the babies. Having received my signal, Juliet proceeded to let the first two dogs out to meet the puppies. Sasha and Sheba came running out as she opened the door for them and almost immediately saw the two tiny bundles in 'their' garden and came to a crashing halt in front of them. Far from being frightened or the slightest bit nervous, Muffin and Petal just stood their ground and wagged their little tails excitedly at the two big, fully-grown staffies that had just run up to them like a pair of express trains.

Sheba was a little unsure of the newcomers, which was normal behaviour for her, and we watched her closely as she sniffed at the pair of them, checking them out. Sasha, on the other hand, walked up to one, then the other, her tail wagging in welcome, and both puppies reacted by jumping up at her with excitement. Sasha hadn't quite reached her second birthday and hadn't yet been afflicted by the canine epilepsy which would later cast a permanent shadow over her life.

Puppy Muffin

Once she saw how well Sasha was getting along with the puppies, Sheba joined in the welcome and was soon touching noses with our new babies and making friends with them. I nodded to Juliet, and she proceeded to let the rest of the dogs out, two at a time, a couple of minutes apart and very soon the puppies were having great fun chasing the bigger dogs around the garden. This was the first time we'd introduced puppies to our pack and the result was a pure joy to behold. All our dogs seemed happy to find two babies amongst them and with the exception of Penny who remained slightly aloof from the newcomers, they were all keen to get to know these two new tiny packmates.

It wasn't long before the two pups, without any encouragement from us, began following Sasha round the garden and when Sasha decided to go back into the house, they trotted along happily behind her, though when she went in through the back door, they needed a little help from us, as their little legs couldn't quite negotiate their way over the doorstep. They now proceeded to explore the utility room and the kitchen, all the time keeping close to each other. They checked out the various dog beds in the kitchen, their little noses appearing to be doing a lot of sniffing at the blankets in the beds. Perhaps they were seeking the reassuring scent of their mother and father, and perhaps their siblings with whom they were used to cuddling up with in the big bed in the kitchen at John and Jane's house.

After leaving them to investigate their new home for a few minutes, Juliet and I were happy when the two pups settled down in one of the beds and curled up together. It had been an exciting morning for them so far, and it wasn't a surprise to see them apparently tired out and in need of some puppy sleep. Imagine our surprise, when, a few minutes later, we checked on the sleepy pair and found Sasha in the bed with them. There she was, sitting up proudly, with a look on her face that seemed to say to us, "These are my babies and I'm taking care of them now."

We could hardly believe what we were seeing. Sasha had been spayed when she was around nine months old, but it appeared to us that she hadn't lost her natural mothering instinct.

"Are you looking after the babies, Sasha?" I said and as if she knew just what I was asking her, she continued sitting protectively with 'her' puppies, but wagged her tail as if in answer to me.

"That's incredible," Juliet exclaimed, as a smile spread

across her face. "Who'd have thought that Sasha would take over the puppies like that?"

It might have been a one-off occurrence, of course, but Sasha would go on to prove us wrong and as the puppies first few days with us seemed to fly past, it became clear that Sasha was taking her new role as 'surrogate Mum' to the puppies very seriously.

Sasha with baby Muffin & Petal

Sasha simply refused to leave 'her' babies and literally devoted herself to taking care of little Muffin and Petal. She did such a marvellous job that we found ourselves having very little to do when it came to house training the puppies. They quickly learned to accept Sasha as their 'new' mum, and they followed her everywhere. When Sasha went outside to go to the toilet, Muffin and Petal dutifully trotted after her and they too went to the toilet. They seemed to learn in no time at all that they weren't allowed to do wees or poos in the house, and neither Juliet nor I can honestly remember ever having to clean up even once after the pair of very good puppies, the first time we've ever experienced such a thing.

At night, Sasha slept upstairs in our bedroom as she'd done since she was a puppy herself, so naturally we fixed the puppies up with a bed in our room as well. Sasha had a large dog bed and when we went to bed, we found the two puppies tended to ignore their own bed and they would snuggle up together with 'Mummy' Sasha. The puppies are now over eight years old, but Muffin and Petal still liked to cuddle up with or close to Sasha at night, so we think it's quite obvious that whatever Sasha did with those two tiny puppies obviously imprinted itself on them to such a degree that they still relied on her to be their comforter and protector even after becoming adult dogs.

So, the two new additions to our doggie family probably settled into our home and its daily routine better than any previous new additions to the family, thanks to Sasha. That's not to say they didn't have a sense of independence and curiosity. In typical puppy fashion their little noses were into anything and everything as they explored their new world, first of all the house and garden and, after having visited our vet, where the staff instantly fell in love with the pair of them, and having their necessary vaccinations, they were ready to explore the big wide world. Before then, however, events were to take place that would add yet another puppy to our happy family of dogs.

Muffin, Sasha and Petal, still sleeping together

3

BETTER LATE THAN NEVER –
ANOTHER ARRIVAL

THE FIRST TWO weeks in Muffin and Petal's lives with us seemed to fly past, as the little girls settled in perfectly and the other dogs all fully accepted them as part of the pack. Sasha continued her surrogate mother role, spending most of her time playing with the puppies and doing whatever she did in terms of 'instructing' them in correct puppy behaviour. It really was quite incredible how much they seemed to learn by being constantly in Sasha's presence.

It was on the fourteenth day of their lives with us that the phone rang one morning. I answered it and was surprised to hear Jane's voice, the lady from whom we'd bought the pups.

"Brian, hello," she began. "Thanks for sending us the latest photos of the puppies. We're so happy they've settled in so well with you and your dogs."

"You're welcome," I replied. "We love them both so much already."

"We know you do, and that's kind of the reason for this call. Yesterday evening, John drove the last puppy to Harworth, to deliver him to his new owners, but when he pulled up outside the house, he was appalled at what he found. The house and garden looked really scruffy and there was rubbish piled high in the garden. There were three really dirty, rough looking kids playing in the mess of the front garden and John took one look and decided that was no place for a little puppy. He left the puppy in the crate in the car and went and knocked on the front door. The man who answered the door asked him where the puppy was. John told him straight that there was no way he was prepared to leave a little puppy in a house that was such a mess. Before the man could say anything, John handed over the deposit they'd left with us when they'd come here to see the puppy, turned around, got back in the car and drove straight home, where he told me what had taken place."

"Sounds like the puppy had a narrow escape," I said, as Jane paused for breath.

"He certainly did," she said. "And that's the reason I'm calling you today."

"Oh?" I was intrigued.

"Yes, John and I sat down and talked about the last puppy. We so much want the little fellow to have a safe, loving home, and that's when John mentioned you and Juliet."

"He did?"

"Yes. He said it was obvious how much you and your wife love dogs and the two girl puppies look so happy in the photos you've sent us. We both agreed that we'd like you to take the last puppy, if you want him, of course."

"Wow, yes, of course I'd love to have him Jane, but I'd need to talk it over with Juliet first, and we can't really afford another new puppy as well as all the expense of the things we'd need."

"We talked about that, Brian, and we don't want the £50 for him. If you can afford a token payment of £20, he's yours, and we know you'll give him a great home."

"Okay, let me have a word with Juliet and I'll call you back in a few minutes," I replied.

When I'd finished the call with Jane, Juliet, who'd heard most of my side of the conversation, had obviously caught on to what I'd been discussing. She expressed her doubts to me.

"We don't even know what he looks like. I can't visualise him from when we visited and picked Muffin, and what about the cost?"

I told her what Jane had said about the price and answered her query about what the puppy looked like quite easily.

"I can drive over there, and if I like what I see, I'll take a photo on my phone and send it to you."

"Well, we don't want him ending up with bad owners," she said, after I'd related the full story of John's visit to the house in Harworth. "I suppose you'd better drive over there and have a look at him."

I called Jane back as promised and within minutes I was in the car heading towards the racecourse once again. When I arrived, John was waiting to greet me at the door and ushered me through to the lounge, where Jane sat, cuddling the puppy on her lap. He was a very handsome puppy with quite striking and unusual markings. He had a white head with a brindle patch over his left eye, with white shoulders and chest, and then a brindle body, that looked so perfectly aligned with the white front that he looked as if he was wearing a brindle coat, tailored perfectly to fit his body. He was instantly friendly, wagging his tail at me as Jane placed him in my arms so I could give the little boy a cuddle. I was already convinced we should have him and handed him back to Jane so I could take a photo of him to send to Juliet. Having sent it, I waited a couple of minutes and before I could call her to make sure the photo had reached her, she called me instead.

"He looks cute," she said. "It's not a very clear picture, but I've seen enough. Bring him home."

That was it. Decision made, I paid Jane and John the £20, and the little boy was ours. He was a very good puppy as I placed him in the rear compartment of the car, instantly sitting down and looking out of the windows (he had longer legs then the two girls). I set off for home giving John and Jane a wave as they saw us off from their front gate, and in minutes, arrived home with our new baby boy.

We went through the usual routine of introducing the other dogs to the new puppy, with one important exception. The first dogs we let out of the house were Muffin and Petal. We wanted to see how they'd react to meeting up with their brother after two weeks apart.

Don't anyone ever tell me that dogs don't recognise each other. As soon as Muffin and Petal saw their brother, they literally pounced on him, tails wagging furiously, doggy kisses lavished on him, which of course he happily repaid. The three puppies were obviously so happy to see each other again and after a minute of this greeting procedure they all ran off down the garden together, happily jumping and leaping around. In short, they appeared to be ecstatic to be together again.

We let the rest of the dogs out to meet the new, as yet un-named new arrival and looking back, it was as if they hardly noticed that another puppy had been added to the previous newcomers. The one exception of course, was Sasha, who immediately recognised the little boy as another baby to add to her 'puppy creche'. Within a short space of time the little fellow was happily following her around, in the company of his two sisters, and despite being a couple of weeks behind the girls in terms of his development he soon picked up the routine of the pack, and like them, never did a single wee or poo in the house. Whatever Sasha did to teach the three puppies to go outside if they needed the toilet, I wish I could package it and sell it to other dog owners. I could make a fortune.

As our new arrival happily settled in with his sisters and the other dogs on that first day, Juliet and I were left with the task of choosing a name for our new arrival. I thought of Patch, for obvious reasons, but Juliet was never one for the ordinary or the obvious. After watching the puppies running around and playing for a few minutes, she announced,

"We'll call him Digby."

"That's a nice name," I replied. "What made you think of it?"

"No special reason," Juliet responded. "It just seems right for him."

"Okay, Digby it is," I agreed, and we spent the rest of the day calling our new puppy by the name Juliet had selected for him, and I could swear that by the end of the day, he knew he was Digby. We had no need of another bed for him, as he simply snuggled up with his sisters wherever they might be, and of course, Sasha quickly took him under her wing, (or should I say 'paw'), meaning he quickly assumed the routine of following his sisters when they followed Sasha into the garden etc. Throughout their early days with us, not one of the three puppies did a single wee or poo in the house and to this day, Juliet and I still find it hard to believe.

At night, Digby joined his sisters in the crate we'd bought for them to sleep in, in our bedroom, next to Sasha's bed. As much as we trusted them, we didn't think it advisable to have them loose in the bedroom while we were asleep, just in case of accidents. We weren't to know at that time that the pups would be so good in the house. I remember the evening of Digby's first day with us. We'd got into the habit of placing the crate, with the door open, in the lounge where they could be with us and the other dogs, who were allowed in with us in the evening, but have somewhere they could feel secure. Muffin and Petal had already got into the habit of curling up together in the crate while we watched the TV or did whatever we had to do in the evening. Juliet waited until the two sisters had made themselves comfortable and then, after giving him a cuddle and a kiss on the top of his head, she placed him gently in the crate beside them. Without a second's hesitation, little Digby snuggled up to his siblings and was asleep in seconds. I think he was glad to be reunited with his sisters.

Those early days which were a new experience for Juliet and me, having three puppies at once in the house, could have been an extremely stressful experience for us, and yet, thanks to the help of Sasha in caring for them, and the fact that they were such fast learners, their first few weeks as a trio were actually completely trouble free. We didn't have one accident in the house, no barking apart from their little play barks, and as soon as Digby was fully inoculated, we would take it in turns to walk the three together to the local playing field, where we'd let them off their leads to play. They were incredible. They needed only minimal recall training, as they would all stick together on the field, and to be honest, they never strayed far from either me or Juliet whoever might be walking them. In fact, it reached a point where I'd wait until they were busy investigating under a bush and then I'd quietly wander off until I'd put maybe thirty of forty yards between us, and then I'd call them, using the one word 'Puppies!' and they'd turn around, see I'd 'left' them and come scurrying back as fast as their little legs could carry them. This ploy wasn't always successful as half the time I tried to walk away, one of them would notice me heading away from them and suddenly, all three would hurry to catch up with me. They really were that good. If you look at the photo of the three of them on the field, you can realise just how marvellous they were, at such a young age to sit so perfectly together, without any of them trying to run away to play.

Muffin, Digby and Petal, Perfect Puppies

Another positive aspect of those early walks on the field was that it gave the puppies plenty of opportunity to socialise and get used to other dogs as we'd invariably meet at least one or two people who would be exercising their dogs and who were usually happy to let their dogs come and say hello to the three pups.

Even people without dogs would come across to talk and make a fuss of the three little dogs. Most of them were intrigued to find someone with three puppies, running around the field, and enjoying themselves off-lead. The question I was asked most often was, "How do you cope with three puppies at once in the house? Don't they make a lot of mess? They would then be surprised when I explained that having the three puppies was in fact no more of a problem than having a single pup. They were generally astounded when I told them we hadn't had a single wee or poo in the house since we'd obtained the puppies. In fact, as I said to one person one day, "It's like having one dog with twelve legs, because they generally do everything together. They all go out to the garden together and if one does a wee, the other two copy them and so on. Sasha's been marvellous with them, and they also follow her around and copy her behaviour."

That description of one dog with twelve legs has stuck with them over the years and it's one we still use to describe them to people.

So, in the space of a few weeks our doggie family had expanded by three, (or twelve legs), and although she would never forget her lovely little Chudleigh, I couldn't help noticing that over the first few weeks of Muffin, Petal and Digby being part of our family, Juliet's mood and general demeanour steadily improved. My idea of getting a new puppy for her to focus on had clearly worked, three times over, and it was almost inevitable that she soon developed an extra-special rapport with Digby, her new little boy. Digby reciprocated her feelings and rapidly became 'Juliet's dog'. He knew she tended to favour him, without ignoring our other dogs of course, but 'Diggers' as we grew to call him, had obviously wormed his way into her heart in no time at all and I was so happy for her. At last, she could put her memories of Chudleigh in a special, private place in her heart without him being constantly to the forefront of her thoughts.

In their own way Digby and his sisters had proved to be the finest therapy Juliet could have received and gradually, her depression over the loss of poor Chudleigh became a thing of the past. She now had three new baby dogs to love, to train and focus her energies on, not forgetting our other dogs of course.

4

PERSONALITIES

IT WAS INEVITABLE THAT, as they grew through their first year of life, our trio of happy pups would begin to display aspects of their own individual personalities. Although they continued to play and do most things together, we gradually noticed various traits which differed from dog to dog. It wouldn't have been normal if they'd all been exactly the same.

To put it in brief terms, we soon identified Muffin to be the comedian, the joker in the pack, and the cheeky one of the trio. If there's mischief afoot you can guarantee Muffin won't be far away. While still little more than a puppy, I caught her one day, fast asleep in the sun, in the back garden, nothing unusual in that of course, but just look what she was using as a pillow. Well, it does say DOG after all...

Sleepy Muffin knows what a bowl saying DOG is for!

Working on the basis that if a bowl says 'Dog' she used it as a pillow, then it surely made sense in Muffin's little mind, that if a cushion was shaped like a circle, that instead of lying ON it, she had to lie AROUND it. Every day, that little dog would find something to do that made us laugh, or at the very least, brought a big smile to our faces.

Moulded Muffin

Digby, despite being the male of the trio was easily identified as the 'wuss' of the three, a bit of a coward, to put it mildly. How did we come to that conclusion? Well, one sunny morning, Juliet called me to come and watch what Digby was doing in the back garden. I joined her at the window and together we watched as he appeared to be stalking something in the garden. We thought it might be an insect or something similar, as our dogs have often turned chasing insects into a game. Digby was watching whatever it was most intently, occasionally adopting a typical play crouch and then rapidly standing up and taking a step back. We decided to quietly sneak outside to try and see what he was so engrossed in. Imagine our faces when we drew closer and saw that the object of his fascination was...a feather! Not just any feather, however. This had to be one of the smallest feathers we'd ever seen. We quietly giggled as we watched him and then, just to demonstrate the effect of the feather on our 'brave' boy, a slight gust of wind blew across the garden and the feather rolled about an inch across the ground. Digby leaped back in terror as this strange and obviously vicious centimetre-long white feather moved in for the attack, and he promptly jumped not to attack the feather, but to get out of its way. The look on his face told us he was terrified of this strange alien thing that had so engrossed him. We couldn't stop laughing at him. To this day, Diggers is terrified of feathers, and whenever he comes across one in the garden he'll go into a crouch and stiffly confront it, never daring to actually touch it. Usually, the situation is resolved by either Petal or Muffin who will go to see what he's doing and one of them will usually pick up and destroy the offending feather.

Poor Digby. We've never been able to work out just what's so terrifying about feathers. Then, we come to his trembling. Digby likes to spend a lot of his indoor time in the utility room, in what we call his 'day bed,' which we placed there specifically for him to relax in during the day. We soon noticed that he would sit up in the bed and visibly tremble, although there was nothing scary anywhere in close vicinity to him. If Juliet or I spoke to him or went to give him a stroke or a cuddle, his little tail would wag furiously with happiness, but he would continue his trembling, despite all the love and cuddles we lavished on him. He still does it today, at eight years old and will even sit beside his Mum or me, closely snuggled up, and we can feel his body trembling. We call it his 'tremblitis' but there's nothing wrong with him. It's just something he does. It's not that he's a nervous dog, far from it, he's super-confident in terms of his general behaviour. He just has these little quirks which if anything, add to his cuteness and makes him even more lovable.

As a puppy he used to love playing games of tug-of-war with Muffin. I'd make a suitable tug-toy out of a few pairs of old socks, (much cheaper than buying toys which would be destroyed in a few minutes), and the two of them would spend ages happily playing their own private tugging games.

Digby and Muffin play tug-of-war, refereed by Sheba,
watched by Dylan

You might wonder where Petal was during all this playfulness from Muffin and Digby. I've saved this short personality description of her till last, as we soon learned that Petal was the most reserved and 'private' of the three puppies. She still enjoyed playtimes of course and could be equally as funny as Muffin and Digby, but she tended to stay more in the background. While Digby soon became very much a 'Mummy's Boy' and Muffin was generally everyone's best friend, Petal, if anything, tended to be more of a 'Daddy's Girl'. She was 'the quiet one' of the trio, the more studious and thoughtful puppy, or so it appeared on the surface.

I soon found that Petal had a rather cute 'smile' that only appeared if she was stroked in a certain way, just behind her shoulder. Her head would go on one side and her mouth would fall into a lovely lop-sided grin, something she does to this day.

She especially loved tummy rubs, and because she had the longest legs of the three pups, she looked really funny and ungainly as she rolled over on her back, legs akimbo, as she waited for her tummy to be rubbed and tickled. In general, of course, she loved to play with her brother and sister in the garden and they would often parade around the garden in single file, as though they were playing 'follow-the-leader'. Petal was also the most inquisitive of the three puppies. She'd stick her nose into anything in order to investigate new smells or new places. Digby always looked as if he had the longest legs, but I think it was because Petal was longer in the body that she didn't appear to be as tall as Diggers.

Wrong way, Digby!

So, those early months with our three beautiful new puppies were a kind of learning curve for us all. Although they were very similar in most ways, we discovered they were each individuals with separate easily definable personalities.

Our other dogs accepted them from day one, without any problems. Sasha continued to 'mother' them while they continued their growth and development. Puppyhood tends to be all too short a period in a dog's life, so we were determined to enjoy the experience of watching and learning as our three new babies negotiated their first year of life.

Having said that, their first year wasn't without a few problems, which we'll meet head-on in the next chapter.

Petal

Cute puppy

5

HEALTH ISSUES

AS THE PUPPIES GREW, it was obvious that they couldn't spend their entire lives together and we gradually began taking them for walks with the other dogs, which they found great fun, as they experienced new playmates and met more dogs as they went for different walks, depending on who they were with at the time. It was during a walk with Sasha and Sheba when Petal was enjoying a good run on the playing field, that I first noticed Petal appeared to be walking and running with a slightly unusual gait, something that hadn't previously been evident during her walks and playtimes with Muffin and Digby. At first, both Juliet and I assumed she'd probably strained a muscle while running and playing with the bigger dogs, but after a week or so, when the problem hadn't gone away, and Petal seemed to be walking and running with a very stiff, straight-legged kind of movement, we decided it might be a good idea to take Petal to the vet.

I phoned our veterinary surgery and managed to get her an appointment for early the following day and she and I subsequently arrived for her appointment. The staff, who hadn't

seen her since she'd attended as a tiny puppy for her inocula-
tions, were so pleased to see her, and made such a fuss of her,
which of course, Petal loved. After all, what five-month-old
puppy wouldn't enjoy receiving lots of love and fuss from three
or four young ladies making her feel like the most important
dog in the world?

We were fortunate to have been given an appointment with
Ben, who would soon become Sasha's vet when she was diagnosed with epilepsy soon afterwards. Ben had specialised in the
treatment of canine epilepsy, having owned an epileptic dog
himself, and he wanted his Daisy to have the best possible treatment. For now, though, his priority was Petal, who he quickly fell
in love with. He adored her eyes, and Petal in return responded
with a furiously wagging tail and allowed Ben to examine her
legs fully, bending and moving them around to assess her joint
movement ability. She loved the attention! After the examination, Ben suspected that Petal might be suffering from elbow
dysplasia and decided to do further tests. I'd heard of hip dysplasia, but this was the first time I'd heard of elbow dysplasia. Ben
explained that they were very similar, just that they affected
different joints. In the meantime, he prescribed a course of
painkillers for Petal, and we left the surgery after making another
appointment in three days' time for the tests to be carried out.

Juliet was surprised when I informed her of Ben's likely
diagnosis. Like me, she didn't think such an illness would be
present in a dog of such a tender age, but I explained to her
what Ben had told me, that it can strike at any age and that in
Petal's case it may be an inherited condition, either from one of
her parents or other ancestors. Sure enough, when the tests
were carried out and the results received, and Petal and I
visited the surgery again, Ben confirmed the diagnosis. Petal
would have to remain on the painkillers for a time, but as she

was still growing there was a chance her joints, which were still in the growth phase, might actually improve in time. The abnormalities present in the joints at that time weren't as serious as they would normally appear in an older dog, so Ben was hopeful for the future.

During the weeks following Petal's diagnosis, she paid regular fortnightly visits to the surgery, where Ben would assess her progress on the painkilling medication he'd prescribed. Her problem had no effect on her running and playing normally, and only someone who was aware of the elbow dysplasia might have discerned that she had a problem, owing to her slight stiffness when walking.

Roly-Poly Petal

About a month after Petal's diagnosis, we couldn't help noticing that her sister appeared to have developed a slight limp while out walking one day. Thinking at first that Muffin had probably pulled or strained a muscle while playing or running around, we didn't worry too much at first. When a week had passed, however and the limp showed no signs of improvement,

Juliet and I agreed a visit to the vet was in order for the second of our two little sisters.

Our appointment was with Ben and even before we went into the consulting room, I was pretty sure what the diagnosis was going to be. Ben gave Muffin a thorough examination and as with Petal, he suggested further tests, suspecting she had the same problem as her sister. Muffin was slightly more nervous than Petal and was quite scared as Ben carried out the examination. Sure enough, when the results came back, Muffin was diagnosed with elbow dysplasia, just like her sister. Although only mild in its manifestation, we would need to watch our little girls closely in future, but for the time being a short course of painkillers and joint support medication seemed to do the trick and the two sisters were soon back to their usual running, jumping and play-fighting.

I did ask Ben, on one of my visits with Muffin, if we could expect the dysplasia to show up in Digby, their brother, as it appeared to be an inherited illness, either from their parents or from further back in their descendants. Ben explained that these things couldn't be predicted. Digby might end up being totally untroubled by the problem, or it could develop at some time in the future. For the time being, we hoped that maybe it would bypass male family members and would be restricted to the female line.

Once the medications kicked in, both Petal and Muffin appeared to make a full recovery from the painful joints, though Petal retained the slightly awkward gait to her walk, which she still has today. We just think it adds something to her cuteness!

As the months passed it certainly made no difference to their abilities to run and play like normal puppies, both in the garden at home, or when out on the open fields on their regular afternoon walks. At least once a day, Juliet would take all three of them together to play and run on the large playing field near our home. She would invariably come home with a big smile on her face as she related to me some of the antics they would display on the field. Chief amongst them was what Juliet described as 'doggy rugby' (minus a ball), whereby the three puppies would chase each other at breakneck speed around the field for a while and then the game would change as Digby and Muffin would take it upon themselves to play a game of 'tag', chasing poor Petal until they caught her, (Juliet suspected Petal 'let' them catch her), and then the two of them would virtually rugby tackle her to the ground, with the two of them piling on top of her, Petal on her back, legs akimbo, as they indulged in a raucous few minutes of play-fighting, until Petal decided it was game over, when she'd extricate herself from the scrum, leap to her feet and set off running across the field with the others following in her wake.

Petal and Muffin play-fighting

Weeks turned into months and the puppies continued to grow and develop normally and we were able to virtually forget the early problems suffered by little Petal and Muffin. Digby seemed to be growing taller as the months passed, and he soon became the tallest of our three siblings. His legs grew longer and longer, and he soon gained the nickname 'Longshanks' from me. (Short history lesson: Longshanks was the name by which King Edward I of England was known, in addition to his more bloodthirsty nickname, The Hammer of the Scots).

Sasha continued to watch over the puppies, particularly Petal and Muffin, with Digby growing up to be more independent and not relying on his surrogate Mum as much as the girls. Despite the two girls having been diagnosed with the elbow dysplasia, Digby was growing up perfectly fit and happy and showed no signs of any discomfort while running and playing. With luck, we hoped he'd not be bothered by the problem in later life. Only time would tell.

Young Digby

6

WHEN THINGS GO WRONG

MUFFIN AND PETAL were approaching their ninth month when the two little girls had their first 'season'. We'd been advised to let them have one season before having the girls neutered, so when they both went through that first season within a couple of weeks of each other, we decided to book them into the vets for the procedure.

Juliet thought it would be a good idea to have them both done at the same time so I duly booked a dual appointment and both pups would be neutered on the same day. It would certainly save having to go through two separate recovery phases after the operation and they should both be back to their playful best at the same time.

I duly made an appointment for the two girls to have the operation on the same day and arrived on the appointed day bright and early, both pups being welcomed with lots of love and affection by the vet's staff and nurses. When the time came to leave them and go home, both Muffin and Petal seemed reluctant to be left at the surgery without me and tried their best to follow me out of the consultation room. Dogs really know how to make you feel guilty don't they?

Both Juliet and I really missed them through the day, but Digby was absolutely distraught. He was whining and crying all through the day, quite clearly, he was missing his sisters, and couldn't understand where they were. He sat in his bed most of the time, trembling and whining, and though Juliet and I did our best to reassure him they'd be home later that day, of course he couldn't understand what we were trying to explain to him.

Just after two pm I called the surgery to inquire as to their progress. The receptionist left me hanging on as she went away to check on them, returning a couple of minutes later with the news that they'd both had their operations and were in recovery, though still a little groggy from the anaesthetic. I was asked to call to collect them at around 5.30 that evening and I couldn't wait to have our two girlie pups back home where they belonged.

At a little after 4.30 pm, I set off for the vet's surgery, anxious to bring my little dogs home as soon as possible. Having arrived, I checked in and took a seat in the waiting room. Luckily, I wasn't kept waiting too long and within ten minutes I was called into one of the consulting rooms by the vet. Rebecca, the vet was accompanied by Helen, one of the veterinary nurses, and two very sleepy-looking puppies. My heart instantly went out to our two baby girls, who both looked so sad and sorry for themselves. Their little tails instantly began wagging when they saw me, though only at about half their usual speed. They were literally wagging in slow motion, but it was plain to see they were both so happy to see me. Little Muffin's togue was sticking out about half an inch, something she always did when she was tired. Petal just looked miserable and worn out.

Like many owners, when collecting their pets after any kind of surgery, I felt immensely guilty for having put my pups through the procedure even though it was a routine procedure and I knew it was for their own good in the long run. Rebecca assured me they'd both been very good dogs and that the operations had gone perfectly well. She told me they would need to return to the surgery in three days for their first post-operative check, gave me a supply of Metacam pain killer to be given to them once a day, starting the following day, and after I'd made the appropriate follow-up appointment at reception, two of the nurses insisted on carrying Muffin and Petal to the car for me, where they gently placed them on the big dog cushion in the rear luggage compartment.

We made it home in about ten minutes, and Juliet was waiting for us and together, we carried the little dogs into the house, before putting them down. Little Digby was beside himself with excitement at seeing his sisters again. His tail wagged furiously, and he made lots of funny little noises which were obviously designed to let the rest of us know how happy he was to have his sisters back home where they belonged.

Together again

Muffin and Petal were so sleepy when they got home, and

obviously still groggy from the anaesthetic. They did, however, eat a little food before they wandered on shaky legs out into the back garden, closely attended by Digby, and by Sasha who was very concerned for them and showing her usual maternal instincts. They were soon dozing in the evening sunshine, where they stayed for a while before coming indoors where they slept most of the evening, only venturing outside once more at bedtime.

Juliet and I each carried one of the pups upstairs at bedtime, Muffin for her, and Petal gently cradled in my arms, not wanting them to pull their stitches by running upstairs as they usually did at bedtime. The following morning, though still not fully recovered from the effects of the anaesthetic, both pups were much more lively and devoured their breakfast as usual which included their first dose of Metacam. Later in the morning, we first noticed that Muffin's operation wound was bleeding. It wasn't a matter of a little seepage either, there was quite a lot of blood. I was immediately concerned. We'd had enough dogs neutered over the years for both Juliet and I to know when there was a problem. I wasted no time, and immediately called the surgery and spoke to Rebecca the vet. She asked me to take little Muffin to see her straight away, and within half an hour of us noticing the bleeding, she was on the examination table once again.

After examining her, Rebecca came to the conclusion that for some reason, the stitches in Muffin's operation wound were literally coming apart, gradually exposing the wound, a potentially dangerous situation, as it would leave our little girl open to infection. They would need to admit Muffin and re-stitch the wound. I had to leave poor Muffin with her so she could be attended to without delay. My poor little girl looked totally crestfallen as I left her there, wondering why she wasn't coming home with me.

The situation reached even greater proportions by the time I arrived home. Juliet immediately asked me to take a look at Petal. Lo and behold, her wound was beginning to leak blood in the same way Muffin's had done earlier in the day.

"Something's definitely not right here," I said, as I explained to her what Rebecca had told me about Muffin and why they'd kept her in.

"You need to take Petal back straight away before they do anything to Muffin," Juliet said with real worry in her voice.

I immediately phoned the vet's surgery and requested that nothing be done to Muffin until I arrived with Petal, who was suffering from the identical problem. Before long, I was back in the surgery with poor Petal, who was bleeding quite heavily from her operation wound. The stitches had literally fallen out and she looked to be in some pain.

Rebecca saw us almost immediately and she was most concerned when she saw Petal's operation wound.

"I've never seen anything like this before," she said, looking quite puzzled. "I can only assume that they've both suffered some form of acute allergic reaction to something in the make-up of the stitches. I'll need to re-stitch the wounds on both girls and use a different type of stitch."

It broke my heart to have to leave our two beautiful puppies at the surgery, so soon after we'd got them home from the operations. Just like Muffin, Petal became really upset when she realised I was leaving the surgery without her. It was the first time I'd ever seen her tail droop and fall between her legs, so I was in no doubt that she was very unhappy at me leaving her.

Rebecca assured me that everything would be okay once the girls were re-stitched, and the wounds closed. I'd known her long enough to take her at her word. I trusted her to help our little girls and put everything right for them. She told me she'd be starting work on the pair of them as soon as possible as a matter of urgency, and that, if all went well, I'd be able to collect them and take them home before the surgery closed that evening. It was still only mid-morning so there was plenty of time for her to sort out both girls, allow them time to come round and recuperate enough for me to transport them in the car. I'd known Rebecca long enough to trust her and accept her word that the pups would be okay after their wounds had been re-stitched.

Once again, Juliet and I faced an anxious few hours as we waited until the appointed time for me to collect the two pups from the surgery. After a phone call to the surgery, confirming that all was well and I could pick them up, I drove once again to the vets and was greeted by receptionist Lisa, who immediately informed me that both pups had been perfect angels during their stay and had been receiving lots of love and cuddles from her, and the rest of the staff. I was soon called in to the consulting room by Rebecca who was waiting for me with both Muffin and Petal, once again both looking very sorry for them-selves and a little groggy from the anaesthetic. She quickly showed me the results of her work on them both. It was clear to see the difference in the stitches. The alternative ones she'd used on this occasion were bright blue in colour, compared to the dark brown ones from the original procedure. She assured me that the wounds had remained clean in both cases and that there was no reason why their recovery shouldn't continue as normal.

It was time to take Muffin and Petal home once again and Rebecca summoned one of the practice nurses, who assisted me in getting both dogs into the car, where they both lay down together on the dog cushion, obviously still quite sleepy and I soon pulled up outside our home as I had done only 24 hours earlier. In a case of déjà vu, Juliet came out to the car to help me take both of our girls into the house where they were once again greeted by Digby, who had again missed his sisters terribly and by Sasha and the other dogs who all wanted to sniff them, (they could obviously smell 'vet' on them), and generally make a fuss around them. All poor Muffin and Petal wanted to do was lie down and go to sleep. With two lots of anaesthetic in two days injected into them, it was hardly surprising and both girls rejected any food and simply slept together in one bed in the kitchen until bedtime, when I had to force them to go out and go to the toilet before we could go upstairs to bed.

Juliet and I again carried one pup each upstairs to bed, where the two girls quickly snuggled up with Sasha, who must have been a form of reassurance to them, as they didn't appear to have moved a muscle when we woke the following morning. Digby had slept in a separate bed beside them, rather than in his usual bed on Juliet's side of the bed. So, Muffin and Petal were surrounded by furry love and warmth all night and in the morning, after we'd carried them downstairs, they both tucked into their normal breakfast after which we administered their dose of Metacam. We looked very closely at the stitches of course, and everything looked fine. There was no bleeding and no undue swelling around the wound site.

Over the next three days Juliet and I watched those stitches like hawks, looking for any signs of the wounds breaking down as they'd done after the first neutering procedure. On Rebecca's advice, we carefully bathed the area around their wounds twice a day with a mild salt and water solution in warm water. By the fourth day, when I returned to the surgery with Muffin and Petal for their routine post-op check, we didn't have long to wait after I checked in at reception to be called into the consulting room where Rebecca welcomed us back yet again to the surgery. She meticulously examined both Muffin and Petal's wounds, paying special attention to the new stiches on both pups. She finally looked up, smiled and professed herself fully satisfied with the outcome.

As if they understood what she was saying, or perhaps just pleased to be receiving lots of fuss from Rebecca, both pups stood on the examination table wagging their tails with happiness and it wasn't long before we were once again on our way home, with an appointment in place to return in a week's time, when hopefully both Muffin and Petal could have their stitches removed. As usual, Digby and Sasha made the biggest fuss when we walked back into the house, with the others also showing their happiness by a profusion of tail wagging and sniffing round both dogs who were obviously carrying that 'vet' smell with them.

This time, there were no problems associated with the stitches and both Muffin and Petal made a full recovery, confirmed by their second post-op check, at which point Rebecca, the vet removed their stitches and gave both dogs the all-clear, and for our two little girls 'normal service' was resumed and they were soon 'back in the groove' running and playing in the garden and on the playing field, as though nothing had ever happened. The trauma of the problems caused by the allergic reaction to the stitches used in their first operations was obviously quickly forgotten and we were able to return to our usual walks and they soon showed their happiness, playing with the doggie friends they regularly met up with on their main afternoon walk.

Feeling better

7

DIGBY'S SURGERY

WITH MUFFIN and Petal finally recovered from their trau-matic experiences, we knew of course that we still had to have our young boy, Digby, 'seen to'. We decided to leave it for another month before booking him in for the procedure, just to give the girls that little bit of extra time to recuperate and get back to their best. Of course, we also hoped there'd be no repe-tition of the problems the girls had gone through when they were spayed.

When the time came to book him in, I phoned and made an appointment and specifically requested that Rebecca carried out the procedure and used the alternative stitches she'd used when Muffin and Petal had been forced to return to have their operation wounds restitched. Obviously, if the girls carried some sort of allergy that had made their bodies reject the orig-inal stitches, there was a good chance that their brother, who shared their genetic make-up, would also reject any use of the standard stitches too. The vets agreed to use the alternative stitches when Digby had his operation and all we had to do now was wait until the day came round and all three of our puppies would then be neutered and we'd be free from the worry of bringing unwanted puppies into the world.

The day before Digby was due to go in for his operation the sun was shining and it was a lovely, warm, autumn day. I still remember walking into the back garden and finding him comfortably relaxing in one of our garden chairs, looking as if he didn't have a care in the world.

Sun worshipping

The following day, I duly set off nice and early and 'Mr Diggers' and I arrived at the surgery at around 8.30 am. Digby's only previous experience of the vets had been the time I took him for his vaccinations, so he had no reason to be nervous when we were called in to the consulting room, but for some reason he was! He trembled like a leaf on a tree branch in a high wind as Rebecca examined him and his tail hung down between his legs. I signed the consent form for the neutering to take place, and one of the veterinary nurses attempted to take Digby out of the room, through to the operating area of the surgery. Poor Digby was shaking as he was led away from me, and he looked back at me as if pleading with me to take him home with me. Did I ever feel guilty? You bet I did.

Rebecca told me not to worry and I knew of course that the staff would make a great fuss of our little boy, until I collected him later that day. When I arrived home without him, both Muffin and Petal instantly realised he wasn't with me and for the rest of the day, the pair were like the proverbial 'cat on hot bricks' and very unsettled, wondering where their brother was. As usual on such occasions, I rang the surgery just after two in the afternoon and was told that Digby had been a really good boy, his operation went without a hitch, and he was awake and had been receiving lots of love and cuddles from all the staff who thought he was a 'gorgeous boy' and they also reported that he hadn't been a moments' bother all day. He'd recovered so well that I could have gone and picked him up straight away, but I decided it would be better for him to rest a little longer before coming home and being surrounded by all the other dogs.

I arranged to call between five and five-thirty and duly arrived soon after 5pm to collect our boy. I wasn't kept waiting long and was pleasantly surprised when a few minutes after I'd taken a seat in the waiting room, the door to the treatment suite opened and one of the practice nurses came walking out with Digby on his lead, who saw me straight away, and his tail went into overdrive, wagging so fast and so hard it looked like a little propeller whizzing around. I think he was pleased to see me. The nurse led me through to one of the consulting rooms and informed me that Digby had been the perfect patient, and that everything had gone perfectly with his surgery. She took pains to point out his stitches, and of course, they were the blue ones, which shouldn't present him with any problems. She handed over a bottle of Metacam painkiller with instructions to give him one dose a day starting from the next morning. She then booked him in for his three-day check-up and that was it, we were good to go. Digby was so excited, and it was hard to guess he'd had anything done to him at all.

As many dog owners will know, neutering for a male dog tends to be less invasive and stressful than it is for females and that was certainly true in Digby's case. With instructions to keep him as quiet and inactive as possible until his post-op check-up, I knew we'd have difficulty keeping him still. On returning home, the other dogs, Muffin and Petal in particular, behaved as if they hadn't seen Mr Diggers for a year, and it was all we could do to stop him from jumping up and down in his happiness to see his sisters after having been separated from them all day.

After surgery, our girl dogs usually weren't particularly hungry, being still under the influence of the anaesthetic. Not so with Digby, who, after going through the greeting process with the rest of the dogs, immediately stood looking at Juliet, who could virtually read his mind.

"I think he wants his tea," she laughed.

"Better not keep him waiting then," I replied with a smile.

Juliet quickly served his tea, placing it on the floor in the utility room, and closing the baby gate to stop the other dogs diving in and joining in his feast. Digby polished the food off in no time and instantly went out into the back garden and did his business, before returning to the house, where he came through to join us all in the lounge. He soon joined Juliet and the other puppies on the sofa, and having made himself comfortable, he promptly fell asleep beside his sisters. The after-effects of the anaesthetic had caught up with him at last and in no time at all he was gently snoring, with his tail giving little wags in his sleep.

Asleep with his Mum and sisters

The following day Digby was up with the lark, bright and early, ready for his breakfast with the rest of the dogs. Apart from being a bit bleary-eyed, we'd never have known he'd had the operation. Poor boy couldn't understand why he wasn't allowed to go for his morning walk as usual, while all the other dogs went out enjoying themselves. He was quite miserable for the next three days: no walks and no running about and playing with his doggie friends. He did try, and once or twice we caught him in the garden trying to jump on Muffin or Petal in his own attempts to encourage them to play with him.

Juliet and I were glad when the third day dawned, and I could take him back to the vet for his post-op check. Rebecca the vet was pleased to inform me that Digby was healing perfectly, and that there were no problems with his stitches. If all went well, I could take him back in another five days' time to have his stitches removed.

Over the next few days, Digby showed no ill effects from his operation, and it was a tough job for us to stop him from going into 'top gear' when it came to playing with the other dogs. He just wanted to run and be his normal self, and sure enough, when I took him back to the surgery for his next post-op check, Rebecca gave him the all-clear.

So, in the space of a few weeks, we'd had all three puppies neutered/spayed, not without some worries over Muffin and Petal, but with Digby being the last of the three to be 'done' we could now relax and let the three of them enjoy life to the full, with no fear of any surprise additions to the family coming along to upset the equilibrium.

8

THINGS CHANGE

THE REST OF THE THREE PUPPIES' first year passed uneventfully. Juliet and I were delighted with our three new additions to the family, though their early days with us certainly hadn't been without the odd drama or two. Perhaps the problems with Petal and Muffin's legs and the traumatic events surrounding their spaying operations helped in some way to make the time appear to fly, and before we knew it their first birthday was upon us.

All three puppies had blended in with the rest of the family, human and canine, and we couldn't have been happier. People would often ask us how we could possibly cope with three puppies to bring up at once, obviously imaging that the three little dogs generated a whole load of work for Juliet and me. As always, we gave the same the identical answer. Bringing up three was no different to bringing up one, as long as the puppies had been properly trained from day one, as was the case with our three. It truly was like having one dog with twelve paws. It really was quite amazing, to see them on a day-to-day basis, no trouble, no petty squabbles; just a real desire from all three of them to enjoy life to the full and loving the constant companionship of their siblings.

As time passed, we gradually saw them begin to form firm friendships with some of our other dogs. They still regarded Sasha as their surrogate Mum, of course, and Sasha remained firmly in charge of the pack and commanded the puppies' full respect at all times. If Sasha stepped in to protest about anything they were doing, the puppies showed instant obedience to her commands. How she communicated with them, we've never really been able to work out. It's something that had to be seen to be believed, but believe me, it's true.

Little Muffin, always full of fun and mischief, was as gregarious as could be, and was happy playing with any of the other dogs, whereas Petal and Digby tended to be more selective in their choice of playmates. Apart from Sasha, Petal's only other regular playmate was, surprisingly, Sheba, while Digby did his best to get Dexter to play with him. Dexter of course, always shied away from doggie games and much preferred either to be alone or surrounded by the wild birds that came to visit our garden. Digby could often be seen adopting the typical play crouch in front of Dexter, who would generally just stare at him with a look that seemed to say, "You must be joking mate."

We began to see other subtle changes in their behaviour around this time. Chief among them was Petal. Usually, she'd go for a walk with me in the morning, with Sasha and Penny. It wasn't a deliberate decision but coincidentally, I found myself walking three black and white dogs, all girls, that drew quite a few comments from various people who'd stop and talk to us on our walk. In the afternoon, she'd walk with Juliet and a couple of the other dogs, when she'd get off-lead and have a good run across the fields or the open space of the larger of our two playing fields. When she'd return home, Juliet would tell me how she had reached a point where she had to warn people not to let small children run up to or try to pet her. She was also very wary of strangers. I was surprised to hear this, as I had no such problems when Petal was with me, with anyone, adult or child being able to approach us and stroke Petal as long as their actions weren't in any way threatening,

It seemed to us that Petal had something of a split personality, quite calm and generally sociable with strangers when she was out walking with me, but with Juliet, she adopted a very defensive attitude towards Juliet. She wasn't the first of our dogs to feel as though they had to 'defend' Juliet against strangers or their dogs. Over the years, we've witnessed similar behaviour from a couple of our dogs and can only assume that Juliet in some way gives off vibes that make the dogs want to protect her from potential threats, even when no threat exists.

Protective Petal

IT WAS around this time when something happened that was to have a profound and ongoing effect on the lives of everyone, human and canine, in our home. One morning, Sasha woke us up about an hour before our usual time of 5.30am. She was at the bedroom door, asking to go out, so I dragged my sleepy body out of bed, threw my dressing gown on and took her downstairs and let her out the back door so she could go to the toilet. After a few minutes, she returned to the back door and walked into the utility room, perfectly normally. What happened next however, was far from normal.

Sasha walked back into the house, and I said, "Okay, Sasha?" as I always talked to her as if she's human, and she just stood next to the radiator, looking a bit strange, is the only way I can describe her appearance. Her legs were trembling, and her eyes had a glazed look about them, and before I knew it, my poor Sasha fell over onto her right side, her legs began 'paddling' in the air as if she was running at top speed, a strange sound came from her throat as if she was being strangled and her mouth was set in an open position, in a horrific-looking rictus. I don't mind admitting it was one of the scariest things I'd ever witnessed in my life. I honestly had no idea what was happening to Sasha, and I called to Juliet who was half asleep in bed, having woken with me when Sasha disturbed our sleep.

"What's the matter," she called to me from the bedroom.

"Something's happened to Sasha," I shouted back to her, and she must have detected the hint of panic in my voice, because without hesitation she shouted, "I'm coming," and within a minute, Juliet had grabbed her dressing gown, and run down the stairs, along the hall, through the kitchen and appeared at my side.

"Oh, my Lord," she exclaimed, on seeing Sasha, who was still in the throes of whatever it was that had suddenly afflicted her. Sasha looked so ill, and we felt helpless to do anything for her and then our poor little dog peed herself as well. Meanwhile the dogs in the kitchen had woken up and could clearly sense there was something wrong, but we couldn't let them in to the room where Sasha was going through what we both suspected might be a stroke or something similar. Whatever it was, it was scaring both of us and Juliet went down on the floor with Sasha and did her best to hold and cuddle her, talking softly and reassuringly to her. The seizure, or whatever it was, seemed to go on for ages, though in fact it was 'only' about five minutes from start to finish, but they were the longest five minutes of my life. Juliet was in tears at the sight of our poor little Sasha apparently suffering her way through this mystery attack.

Gradually, the leg movements slowed down, and Sasha's face returned to normal. Juliet continued cuddling and loving her and I joined her on the floor, adding my strokes and cuddles, just wanting Sasha to get better.

"After all she's gone through already…" I said, not needing to finish my sentence, as we both knew what Sasha had endured in her first year of life, being abandoned, and almost dying in a gutter from hypothermia, and then after we'd rescued her, two broken legs in her first year, as well as the skin allergies that have stayed with her to this day. Now there was something else for us to worry about, and because it was so early in the morning, there was little we could do until the vets opened at 8.15 am.

Then, almost as suddenly as it had started, the seizure or whatever it was ended, and Sasha, though rather groggy and shaky, got to her feet, much to our delight. Her eyes still had a strange look about them, and it was evident to both of us that she was far from normal, despite being up on her feet again. Having said that, Sasha's tail began to wag, a sure sign that she was coming back to her normal self again. She looked at me and I said something to her, what, I don't remember, and then she licked my hand, and I knew my special girl was feeling better.

Juliet and I were still very worried as to the cause of the strange manifestation, and as soon as the vet's surgery was open, I was on the phone to them. I explained what had taken place to the receptionist, who went away, leaving me hanging on for a minute, and then returned, told me she'd spoken to the vet, and asked me to take Sasha into the surgery without delay.

Juliet helped me to load Sasha into the rear of the car and I was soon on my way, arriving at the surgery within ten minutes of leaving home. I was only kept waiting a couple of minutes before being shown into one of the consultation room, where Rebecca, the practice manager and senior vet was waiting for me. We soon had Sasha up on the examination table, where Rebecca gave Sasha the most thorough examination I'd ever seen a dog undergo. She was clearly leaving nothing to chance. Next, she called one of the nurses and between them, they took Sasha through to the treatment suite, where they carried out blood tests which they would analyse urgently. When she came back to the consultation room with Sasha, my little girl was walking a little better, though she still had a sort of glazed look about her eyes.

Rebecca then gave me the devastating news that she was pretty sure Sasha had suffered an epileptic seizure. All the symptoms I'd described pointed to that diagnosis. To say I was shocked would be an understatement. Our poor Sasha was still only two years old and had already been abandoned, almost dying from hypothermia, then after we'd rescued her, she suffered two broken legs in her first year and then been diagnosed with skin allergies. Now, life appeared to have thrown another obstacle in her way. Rebecca then explained as much as she could about the effects of canine epilepsy and the various treatments that were available. Initially she'd start Sasha on a low dose of medication in the hope that it would help prevent repeat seizures.

Rebecca booked us in for a follow-up appointment in one week as she wanted to check how Sasha was doing, by which time they'd also have the results of the blood tests back from the lab. Before setting off for home, I rang Juliet from the car, as I knew how worried she'd be, waiting for news.

"I thought it might be that," she said when I told her Rebecca's diagnosis. She made a big, big fuss of Sasha when we got home, and we determined there and then to do all we could to see her through this latest crisis in her life. As those who've read Sasha's story will know, our gorgeous girl once again proved herself to be the ultimate survivor. Her first two years as an epileptic saw her suffer from many, many 'cluster fits' where she'd have three or four seizures, virtually one after the other, culminating in a terrible occasion when she suffered 14 fits in the space of a day, and had to be admitted to dog hospital. We honestly never thought she'd come home to us after all she went through, but in true Sasha-like fashion, she walked out after three days with a big Staffy smile on her face, as if nothing had happened. The wonderful smiley-face photo used on her book cover was actually taken by a veterinary nurse on the day I collected her after her treatment for the multiple seizures.

It was around that time that a new vet arrived at the practice. Ben had an epileptic dog of his own and had made the illness his speciality in order to help his own dog. He loved Sasha, her spirit and determination, and he set out to teach me all he could about canine epilepsy so that we could do the best we could for her. Without his help, Sasha's life would have been a lot worse. On one occasion he told me, "Brian, I just want you to be aware that Sasha probably won't live a full life span." That was hard news to take on board, but at least he was being honest. Perhaps due to her own doggedness, and fighting spirit, it's so rewarding to be able to say that Sasha celebrated her ninth birthday before disaster befell her.

A friend of mine, fellow author Linda A Meredith, sent me a photo of Sasha, with what she thought would be a perfect motto for our never-say-die staffy girl, and I agreed that it summed up Sasha's spirit in a nutshell. That photo is reproduced below, and it really sums up the wonderful character trait that helped make Sasha the very special dog she was.

Of course, on the day of her diagnosis, the rest of our dogs were just very happy when I arrived home with Sasha and she was greeted by multiple tail-wagging and excitement from all our dogs, especially her three 'surrogate' puppies, Muffin, Digby and Petal. Sasha lapped up the attention they lavished on her and we were just glad to have her home after a very scary few hours.

The story of Sasha's life from the time she was abandoned in a gutter and left to die, to her fight against her terrible illness and all that happened in-between, is told in the first book in this series, the award-winning bestseller, *Sasha*.

But now, we'll return to the story of our three inseparable puppies.

9

MUFFIN'S WANDERLUST

BY NOW OF COURSE, our three puppies were fully grown adult dogs, although to this day we still refer to them collectively as 'the puppies'. They were fully used to walking with any other members of our canine family and it was rare that all three would go on walks together. Usually, as she was the most independently minded of the three, Petal would walk with me, Sasha and Penny in the morning and with Juliet and any two of the others in the afternoon. Muffin and Digby really loved playing together when out for a walk so we tried to keep the two of them together as much as possible. Both were well behaved when let off their leads and could be trusted to have a good run around the playing field, either with each other, or interacting with other dogs...or could they?

I remember only too well the day Juliet returned from a walk with Muffin and Digby and the first words out of her mouth as she walked in through the gate were, "Go on, get in there you naughty girl."

I was shocked, to say the least. She could only be talking about Muffin, who'd never incurred her wrath before.

"What's Muffin been up to?" I asked as she closed the gate behind her and unclipped the dogs from their leads.

"The naughty little thing only ran off from the field," she replied.

"What? Little Muffin?" I could hardly believe what I was hearing.

"Yes, little Muffin," she answered my question with the only possible reply.

"What happened?"

"Everything was okay. She and Digby were playing with Rusty and a couple of other dogs, and I was talking to Pat, (Rusty's owner), and only turned my back for a minute. When I looked again, there was no Muffin. I called her name but there was no response, and you know she always comes back when she's called. Pat suddenly pointed and said, "There she is," and sure enough I just caught sight of her back end disappearing through the exit into the housing estate behind Tesco."

What we refer to as the 'Tesco Estate' is a sprawling labyrinth of new-build homes, with twisting and turning streets, designed to help keep traffic speeds down. Unfortunately, such a design makes it a lot harder to search for a runaway dog, and poor Juliet knew that Muffin could be anywhere in that maze of streets. Quickly clipping Digby on his lead, the two of them set off to search for Muffin.

"We wandered the streets, with me shouting Muffin's name, for about ten minutes," Juliet told me, "And the longer it went on the more worried I was becoming. The traffic on the estate can be quite busy at times and Muffin isn't exactly very street smart, is she?"

I just nodded a silent agreement and motioned for her to go on with her tale.

"I was getting really worried and frustrated, when all of a sudden, I saw this little black shape in the distance. It was naughty Muffin, of course and she must have seen me and Digby because she suddenly set off running towards us at top speed. As she drew closer to us, I could see her tongue was lolling out and her tail was held straight out at the back as though she'd streamlined her body shape for speed. In what seemed like only a few seconds the little minx was skidding to a halt in front of me. She sat at my feet, looked up at me and wagged her tail furiously, as if to say, *"Aren't I a clever girl?"* I was so relieved that she was safe that I couldn't be angry with her and was just happy to have her back. I quickly clipped her lead on to her collar and together, she, Digby and I made our way through the streets towards home. As we walked, I gradually found myself growing angry with the naughty little girl, who was trotting along happily at my side, and then I shouted at her, telling her what a bad dog she'd been, but of course, Muffin hadn't got the faintest idea what I was talking about." Juliet paused for breath, and I looked at Muffin, her tail happily wagging, and fully understood why Juliet couldn't really get angry with her. She was a dog, after all, and she'd simply seen an opportunity to release some pent-up energy and she'd grasped it with all four paws!

The only problem we now had, of course, was that Muffin couldn't be fully trusted when she was let off her lead. For the next couple of weeks Juliet restricted her to lead walks, before finally allowing her off-lead once again. She seemed to have got over her temporary wanderlust and was quite happy and content to run and play with Digby and whichever other dogs were present on the playing field with their owners, until…a couple of months later, she did it again!

Same exit from the field, and with no warning, she did her disappearing trick once again. Luckily, on this occasion Juliet was quite close to the little scamp as she disappeared through the alley from the field to the housing estate, and she and Digby immediately took off in hot pursuit, being able to keep Muffin in sight as she set off into the housing estate. Before she'd gone too far, Muffin turned her head and noticed Juliet and Digby following her, and for some reason, she came to a sudden halt, whereupon she just waited patiently for Juliet and Digby to catch up to her. Once again, Juliet clipped her lead on, and led her back through the housing estate, around the playing field, arriving home in no time at all.

So, once again, Muffin was in bother. Shouting at her would have been fruitless of course. No way would she have understood what Juliet was saying to her and would possibly have made her reluctant to return to Juliet when she called her in future. The only solution we could arrive at, after a long discussion on the 'Muffin situation' was to completely change Muffin's walking routine. Remove the housing estate and the playing field from the equation, and we'd remove the temptation for her to run away in order to carry out her 'private investigation' of the estate.

From the next day, Juliet devised a new afternoon walk for Muffin and Digby. Instead of the playing field, where the dogs could meet and play with their doggie friends, she set off in a completely different direction, heading towards the woods on the outskirts of the village. Returning home almost an hour later, she reported complete success. Muffin and Digby had thoroughly enjoyed their new walk; running and playing in the woods, dashing in and out of the trees and bushes that grew in abundance there. Juliet enjoyed it too, playing hide and seek with the two dogs, as she hid behind a tree, and then called one or both dogs names, and they had great fun running around in search of her, then showing great excitement as they found her hiding place when she'd reward them with a tasty treat.

Juliet enjoyed the new walk so much that she started taking the other dogs down the same route, and so, thanks to Muffin's wanderlust, a new and improved walking routine came into being. As Juliet said, running around in the woods was far more interesting for the dogs, who sometimes got the chance to chase squirrels, (never catching them of course), rabbits, (same results), and generally had a much better time than they used to have by sticking to the playing field and its surrounding area. Over the years, she's continued with the walk in the woods and has even expanded it by finding a path that leads across the open fields to the next village. The dogs love it, and Muffin has never 'done a runner' while on her new walk. Nowadays, the only time she goes on the playing field is when Juliet, for what-ever reason, takes her dogs for a shorter, lead walk.

The Great Escaper!

* * *

WHILE WE'RE TALKING about Muffin, I should tell you that it was around this time in her life that she first began 'talking' to us. I've been trying to think of the best way to describe this comical trait of hers. From being a very young puppy Muffin had always had the habit of what we called 'clacking', where she'd sit in front of someone and open and close her mouth, making a 'clacking' noise with her teeth. It was funny to see her doing this and of course, we'd say words like, "What are you telling us, Muffin?" Her reply was to 'carry on clacking.' Is that a good film title?

As she approached her third birthday however, she suddenly took her communication skills to a new level. One evening as we were sitting in the lounge, watching TV, Muffin jumped up on the sofa, which was quite normal for her to do. She sat on Juliet's legs, facing her, ready for another 'clacking' session. This time however, Muffin surprised us both by actually making a new sound. She looked straight at Juliet and began making strange sounds, (this is the difficult bit), a little like *'arr, arr, ruff, ruff, aaaww, arr arr.'* We could hardly prevent ourselves from laughing. Little Muffin looked so serious as she made these odd sounds, and of course, Juliet responded to her by saying, "What, Muffin? What are you telling me?"

Much to our surprise, Muffin made another series of the same kind of sounds. She continued this vocal communication for well over thirty seconds, her tail wagging all the time. Juliet and I just looked at each other and shared a smile and a quiet laugh.

"She's trying to tell you something," I said.

"I can tell that," Juliet replied. "But what it is, I don't know."

Juliet gave her a big cuddle and said, "I'm sure whatever it is, is very important, Muffin, but I haven't any idea what you're trying to tell me."

This rather strange human/canine 'conversation' continued for what must have been about a minute, after which Muffin decided she'd said all she wanted to say, and she jumped down from the sofa and incredibly came across the room to where I was seated in the armchair, and proceeded to start a whole new dialogue, this time with me!

Having realised that this new form of communication guaranteed getting our attention, Muffin decided that this was fun and from that day through to today, we are regularly regaled by Muffin's 'stories' which can last from a few seconds to a minute or more. She obviously derives great fun from engaging with us in this way. I just wish we could work out what she's attempting to tell us.

There's absolutely no doubt that of the three puppies, Muffin is the definite joker in the pack. Her antics are always guaranteed to have us smiling, or better still, laughing fit to burst. Muffin's version of dog roly-poly has us laughing every time she indulges in it. She rolls onto her back, legs in the air and then proceeds to rock back and forth on her back whilst kicking her legs up in the air, as she twists her body and tail from side to side. No ordinary roly-poly for our Muffin, no way!

She can even make us laugh when he's asleep. She has a habit of falling asleep and the deeper she sleeps, the more the tip of her tongue begins to protrude from her mouth. It just looks so cute and so funny. She's a real little star.

So, there we have Muffin in a nutshell. It's quite funny how three pups from the same litter can have such diverse personalities, as you'll see as we move on to talk about Petal.

10

LITTLE MISS SNOOTY

HAVING TOLD of Muffin's personality in more detail, it's only fair that I do the same for the other members of the trio. Beautiful Petal couldn't be more different from her sister. While Muffin is the definite joker in the pack, Petal is far more serious-minded, though just as lovable. She has a certain look about her, as though she's always indulging in serious thoughts about something. She often sits in the garden, her nose in the air, a habit that gave rise to her 'Little Miss Snooty' nickname. She's actually so lovable, but anyone would think she's looking down her nose at them.

Miss Snooty

Petal has always loved to join in at playtime with Muffin and Digby. Together, they love playing games of rough and tumble, play-fighting and chasing each other round the garden, or if out on one of their afternoon walks, the action is transferred to the big playing field near our home. They take it in turns to chase one dog, like a game of 'tag' and when the two chasers catch up with their quarry, they virtually 'rugby tackle' their victim to the ground and it's hilarious to watch them rolling around on the ground in a tangle of legs, bodies and tails. Anyone who didn't know them could be forgiven for thinking they were witnessing a dogfight, as the noises the three of them make would make anyone think they were engaged in a fight to the death, rather than playful fun. They literally grab each other's legs, collars and anything they can grab hold of with their teeth. The amazing thing is that nobody gets hurt, and when one dog decides they've had enough, they somehow extricate themself from the general melee of wriggling canine limbs and stand still a couple of yards away, and the other two take this as signal that the game is over.

For reasons unknown to Juliet and me, it's usually Petal who calls an end to the rough and tumble. Perhaps it has something to do with the fact that of the three, Petal is definitely the 'wimp' of the trio. If in the course of playtimes one of the other dogs accidentally catches her leg or some part of her body with their teeth, Petal will squeal and try to back away, and if possible, she'll run to Juliet or me and 'put on' a wonderful 'dying swan' act, holding the 'injured' paw up as if to say, "Look what they've done to poor little me."

We then make a fuss of her, rub the leg or paw 'better' and Petal then wags her tail as if to say, "everything's okay now" and off she goes and joins in the game again. Dogs, honestly!

Because of the problems she suffered with her joints in her younger days, she's always retained her slightly unusual 'stiff' gait when walking and when she turns around, it looks as if she has a stiff back and she has a rather awkward turning circle, very wolf-like. If you know wolves, you'll know what I mean.

Perhaps the most endearing thing about Petal is her fur. She possesses the softest, silkiest fur I can ever remember feeling on a dog. Stroking her is really like stroking a silk or satin blouse or skirt, especially on her head. Not only does she look smooth and sleek, but her fur also has what appears to be a 'Teflon-like' quality. You can imagine how dirty the dogs get when the weather is wet and they come home from playing, either on the playing field, or perhaps having had a run in the farmer's field on the outskirts of the village. Petal though, can walk into the house looking like she's spent a week down a coal mine, yet in a few minutes and after a brief rub down with a towel, her coat is pristine once again, as if she'd never been all muddy just a few brief minutes ago. I wish all our dogs could have fur like Petal.

As the three pups grew into adult dogs, the two girls retained their closeness to Sasha, while Digby gradually became less dependent on her. Petal in particular would always stay close to Sasha and would join in one-on-one games with her, which Sasha loved of course, and at night, Petal would claim the right to sleep closest to Sasha. To see the two of them rolling around in the lounge in an evening was so amusing, especially when Sheba would try to join in their game. Sheba is so ungainly when she manages to roll over on her back and it really added to the humour of the moment.

Bedtime for Petal and Sasha

The one thing everyone agrees on is how beautiful Petal is. Her markings which led to us calling her by the name Petal in the first place are so striking and her one black and one white ear give her a really cute look. When seen directly from the front, she looks like a pure white dog with a pretty little button nose, and it's not till you see her from the side that her full markings become apparent. She also has a way of looking at a person that gives her a 'regal' appearance and more than one friend has often referred to her as 'Princess Petal.'

Princess Petal

Then again, some people think she has a permanently 'sad' look on her face. We prefer to think she just looks very serious. Either way, she's a much loved and fun-loving little lady, though not as mischievous as her sister. Which leads me to mention one really endearing fact about our three 'puppies' though of course by now they were adult dogs, but even now we still refer to them as 'the puppies'. It's that it is virtually impossible to stroke or cuddle one of them without the other two suddenly arriving expecting the same treatment. I was reminded of this a couple of minutes ago when Juliet arrived home from a walk with Muffin and Digby and I bent down to give them both a stroke and all of a sudden a third little head poked its way into our loving huddle as Petal, not wanting to be left out, simply barged her way in, and I was left trying to give equal love and affection to three dogs, with only two hands to do it with.

Of the three dogs, Petal is the one who most resembles Sasha and from her puppy days, almost everyone has asked us if Sasha was her mother. The way they acted, it would be a natural assumption to make, and people were surprised when we'd tell them they're not related at all, but that Sasha did 'adopt' them when they were tiny pups and played a big part in raising them in her own way.

11

MUMMY'S BOY

THEN OF COURSE there's Digby, who can only be described as a 100% 'Mummy's Boy,' which I'm sure you'll remember from earlier in the story. At this point it's worth elaborating on that point. Although the three 'puppies' are now adult dogs, they still like to do virtually everything together, making them almost inseparable.

The one way they differ, however, is in the fact that Digby soon latched onto Juliet from an early age and once in the house, he would always make a beeline for her and want to be near her as much as he possibly could. For example, after a walk, while Petal and Muffin would be content to come home, have a drink and flop into a bed for a rest, Digby would stay close to Juliet. If she sat down at the kitchen table with a drink, she'd suddenly find Digby by her side, and he would invariably use those long legs of his to put his paws up and rest them on her lap and would stay there until she'd given him a good stroke on his head and made a fuss of him. Eventually he'd leave her in peace, but not until he'd had his extra share of love and cuddles.

Cuddles on the sofa

Digby's certainly loved up to his nickname 'Longshanks' being tall enough when he stands tall on his back legs to reach the kitchen counter tops, so we have to make sure nothing that might tempt him is left too close to the edge, otherwise it will suddenly 'disappear' into thin air, (or Digby's tummy to be more precise).

Perhaps you might think that his long legs would give him an advantage when running with his sisters, but in fact, he has a long, loping stride when running and isn't as fast as you might think. In fact, little Muffin is the fastest of the three. When she gets into her stride, her little legs literally eat up the ground and from behind all you can see is her hind legs pumping away as she zooms along, easily leaving Digby and Petal in her wake. Petal of course, usually brings up the rear. Little Miss Snooty doesn't really like high-speed running races. Perhaps they're not really Princess Petal's thing.

At bedtime, the three pups, plus Sasha of course, have always slept in our bedroom. While Sasha, Muffin and Petal were quite content with their own beds, Digby long ago decided that his long legs gave him a distinct advantage over the others. He could actually jump up and get on our bed, the cheeky little chap. Following our usual bedtime routine, after we've let all the dogs out for their last chance to go the toilet etc, Juliet goes to the bathroom, having first let the four 'bedroom' dogs go upstairs and into the bedroom to settle down in their beds. I lock up downstairs and make sure the rest of the dogs are in bed, an easy job as they all quickly snuggle down in their beds in the kitchen, with Cassie and Penny sleeping in the lounge.

One night, as I was about to join Juliet upstairs, she called to me.

"Brian, you must come and look at this."

"Why? What's happened?" I replied.

"Just come and see for yourself," she said.

Wondering what I was about to find, I made my way upstairs, walked into our bedroom and instantly burst out laughing. Sasha, Muffin and Petal were all cosy in their beds, but there was Digby, happily enjoying himself, snuggled down on our bed. Not just anywhere on the bed though. He was lying across Juliet's pillow, obviously attracted to his Mummy's scent.

"What are you doing on my bed, cheeky boy?"

It was so funny to see him there, looking at us and acting as if he owned the bed and it was perfectly normal for him to be there. He was so good though, because after we'd finished chuckling at his sheer cheek, as soon as Juliet told him to get down, he jumped down and snuggled up in his own bed, which is right beside Juliet's side of our bed, so he can be close as can be to his Mummy while he sleeps. Occasionally, he leaves his own bed at some time in the night, and we've discovered him, on my side of the bed, cuddled up with either Muffin or Petal. Maybe he fancies a change from time to time.

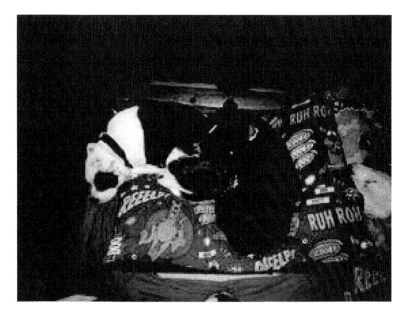

Asleep with Muffin

Those long legs come in handy at other times too. When Juliet has her lunch each day, she always finishes off with a yoghurt of some description. From an early age, all three pups clearly enjoyed the taste of those various yoghurts, because Juliet would hold her empty pot down towards them and three eager little tongues would squeeze their way into the pot to lick out whatever flavour remained within. As they grew to adult size, Digby found himself with an advantage over his sisters. He knew when his Mum was having her yoghurt and in an attempt to be first in the queue for 'licking rights' he'd walk up to sit beside Juliet's chair and when he thought the time was right, he'd suddenly get up and place his paws on Juliet's lap, wagging his tail, asking for his taste of her yoghurt pot. Realising what he was doing, Muffin and Petal would arrive and had no option other than to wait behind him as he had first taste of the yoghurt of the day! A little way off in the future, this little ritual underwent a rather big change as you'll read about soon, but for now, Digby was always first in line for the little lunchtime treat.

Without a doubt, Digby is a happy little chap, and no more so than when he's strutting down the road beside his Mum, usually with either Muffin or Petal, ready for playtime on the field, or perhaps going exploring in the local woods. He also has a habit of pulling some really funny faces in his sleep. It's not always possible to obtain a good photo of him while he's pulling one his funny faces but one day, I managed to get the following photo of him as he was snoozing close to Juliet on the sofa one evening.

Snoozing on the sofa

Of course, before the snooze, there's the yawn, and boy, can Digby yawn. His mouth seems to stretch so far open; he looks as if he's ready to swallow another dog!

The yawn!

So that's a brief summing up of the Mummy's boy, our beautiful Digby, who for some reason is also known by the affectionate nicknames of 'Digbydoo' or 'Diggers'.

12

A NEW PLAYMATE, BUT A FRIEND DEPARTS

SHORTLY BEFORE CHRISTMAS three years ago, Juliet and I were just getting ready to feed the dogs one afternoon. By now, the two girls, Rebecca and Victoria had grown to adulthood, both being in their late teens. Rebecca had successfully gained a place at Leeds University, while Victoria was working for an insurance company.

This particular day, the front door opened, and Victoria walked into the house and immediately said to Juliet, "Mum, you need to come outside, now."

Thinking something was wrong, Juliet's immediate reaction was, "Why, what's happened? We're just doing the dogs' teas."

"Nothing's happened, but you need to come outside, right away, please."

Not knowing what to expect, Juliet disappeared out through the door with Victoria, while I tried to contain my own thoughts on what it could be about as I continued to prepare the dogs' afternoon meal.

It might have been five or maybe ten minutes later when Juliet and Victoria quietly came back into the house. Juliet walked along the hallway towards me holding something in her arms, and I saw…a puppy!

"What's that?" I exclaimed, stupidly, as it was quite obvious what the little bundle in Juliet's arms was.

"Victoria says she's my Christmas present," Juliet replied. "Her name's Honey."

"Oh, is it now?" I said, feeling a tinge of anger. Victoria had been asking for some time whether we could get another dog, but Juliet and I had decided that the ten dogs in our pack were enough to cope with and we kept telling her that the answer was no. Obviously, knowing what we'd told her, Victoria had cleverly decided to get around our refusal by presenting us with a 'fait accompli'.

Despite our initial reluctance, who could possibly not fall in love with the tiny puppy Juliet now held in her arms? She was such a small, cute little thing, honey-coloured, hence the name Victoria had already given her. Apparently, Honey was one of a litter of puppies raised by one of her friends' families and Victoria had reserved her from the day she was born. As she followed her Mum through the door Victoria was carrying a lovely bed she'd bought for the puppy complete with toys, including a little teddy bear that Honey loved snuggling up with, especially at night.

Our chief concern was how the other dogs would react to the sudden appearance of this newcomer in the house. We didn't have much choice and had to go ahead and introduce Honey to the pack. They were already on the alert, having obviously sensed the scent of a puppy on the premises. We tried to introduce her carefully to the others, but they weren't having any of it. They all gathered around Juliet, curious to see this new baby in their midst. As they all seemed to be calm and friendly, we tried to be careful, separating the dogs into two groups of five at time in the room and with our fingers crossed, Juliet placed Honey on the floor.

It was instant love as far as our other dogs were concerned. Sasha, Muffin, Petal, Digby and Penny all took to Honey right away, with lots of sniffing, tail wagging and nose touching. Sasha especially, was enamoured with the new puppy and as time passed, she behaved exactly as she had with Muffin, Digby and Petal, basically 'adopting' Honey and acting as a surrogate mother to the puppy. If Sasha had accepted her, everyone else had to do the same.

Honey

There were no problems introducing Honey to the rest of the pack and we could hardly believe it had all gone so smoothly.

Before we knew it Sasha had completely taken Honey under her wing and was acting the role of mum, making sure Honey was safe and warm, and leading her out in the garden and basically teaching her how to behave in and outside the house. As she had done with the three puppies, Sasha was amazing, and it made the job of house-training Honey so much easier. In fact, just like the three puppies, Honey never peed or soiled in the house, thanks to Sasha.

Juliet and I were amused when I asked Victoria, "What about her injections and insurance?" and Victoria assured us that she would pay for the puppy's insurance and her vaccinations. I gave Juliet a knowing look and in the next few days I arranged for Honey to receive her initial vaccinations, taking advantage of our vets 'Vac for Life' offer, which meant that for a single payment of £99, Honey would receive her annual vaccinations for the rest of her life with nothing else to pay. I also arranged insurance for her with the same company we insured our other dogs with. I'm still waiting to be recompensed. If I could put a smiley face here, I would do so! Never mind, the thought was there, and as they say, it's the thought that counts.

A very happy Sasha with 'her' new adopted baby, Honey

So, Honey grew up in a perfect happy environment. Sasha literally spent hours with her, and it was never too much trouble for Sasha to play with the tiny puppy. The two of them would play together, do 'zoomies' around the house and garden, share in games of 'chase' as first Sasha would chase Honey and then they'd switch roles and Honey would be the chaser, kind of like a game of 'Tig'. Indoors, they'd play games of roly-poly in the lounge, Honey would leap all over the long-suffering Sasha, chew her legs as if they were tasty bones, and those puppy teeth of hers were so sharp, those nips must have hurt, but Sasha never complained or snapped at Honey.

Once she'd had her second round of vaccinations and it was safe to let Honey venture out into the big wide world, our little puppy attracted a lot of attention when she went for her first few walks. People would ask "What breed is she?" and we answered honestly that we didn't really know. It was obvious she was a crossbreed and that she had some Staffy in there somewhere but as for the rest, who knows? We soon noticed that as she grew, Honey seemed to get longer and longer but she didn't actually grow much taller. In fact, we became convinced that somewhere in her ancestry she must have dachshund genes. I used to joke when anyone asked me about her breed, that she's a 'draught-excluder terrier' because if she grew much longer, we'd be able to put her across the bottom of a door to prevent draughts creeping into the room!

As she continued to grow Honey sort of 'discovered' the joys of playing with Muffin, Digby and Petal. Pretty soon, our 'terrible trio' became, 'the fantastic four' as Honey virtually permanently attached herself to the grown-up puppies. It became a great source of entertainment for us to watch them zooming round the garden, the kitchen and once they got on the nearby playing field, it was nothing short of amazing to see them playing together. It really was nothing short of a miracle that none of them got hurt during those playtimes, as to say they were incredibly rough with each other would be a complete understatement.

Honey posing with Digby and Muffin

Another thing that quickly became apparent was the fact that young Honey was not only extremely photogenic, she was also a natural poser. Point a camera at her and she'd instantly assume a perfect pose, as a result of which I could probably fill the rest of this book with nothing but photos of 'The Honey Monster' as I dubbed her. Like most puppies, she was fairly quiet in the first few weeks of growing up. Apart from the usual little puppy squeaks and squeals she was hardly heard until one day, while the dogs were all outside in the garden Juliet and I heard the sound of a dog barking. Now, that's not exactly unusual in a home with eleven dogs, but this was unusual as neither of us recognised the bark we were hearing.

"What was that?" Juliet asked.

"Your guess is as good as mine," I replied. The barking continued and Juliet and I together made our way into the back garden and were amazed to see and hear little Honey barking at the birds on the bird table. The bark was what astounded us. To hear her, you could have been forgiven for thinking you were hearing a Rottweiler or a Doberman Pinscher. It was so loud, deep and throaty. We could hardly believe that sound was coming from that little, tiny body. We were soon to hear more of Honey's voice as she soon began using it during playtimes with the other dogs. I'd like to say that over time, we grew accustomed to Honey's unusually loud bark, but seriously, it still astounds us and makes us laugh to hear that deep, sonorous bark coming from such a small, cute dog.

So, Honey became a much-loved member of our pack and even Sheba, who by now had begun to suffer quite badly from osteoarthritis, did her best to join in and play with the newest member of our canine family.

It was soon after Honey's first birthday however, that a rather heavy, black cloud first manifested itself above our happy pack. Our beautiful staffy/Labrador, Dexter, began to slow down and show signs of not being well. To cut a long story short, Dexter was diagnosed with heart and lung problems and was placed on medication. Walking gradually became difficult for him as he'd get out of breath and needed to stop for short rests during his walks. Anyone who's read my earlier book, *Remembering Dexter* will know that poor Dexter eventually passed away in my arms a year later, and his life is commemorated in my book of his life and in the memorial garden we created in his memory, as Dexter was an unusual dog in that he loved the wild birds that visited our garden every day, even allowing sparrows to perch on his back as he lay in the sun near the bird table. Dexter's Memorial Garden is not only a place where the birds come to feed, but also serves as a protective sanctuary against neighbourhood cats. Dexter was especially missed by Muttley, usually a loner within the pack who looked on Dexter as his best friend. It took Muttley a long time to get over the loss of his friend, but eventually, who else but Sasha, took it upon herself, to take over the 'job' of being Muttley's best friend.

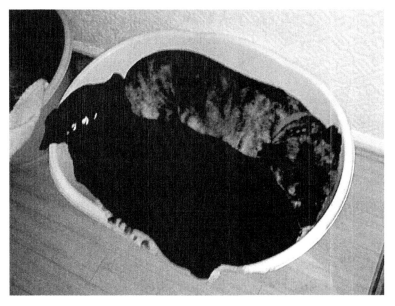

Dexter's last night, cuddled up with Muttley

One thing's for sure, Dexter will always be in our hearts and will certainly never be forgotten. There was one strange consequence following Dexter's passing over the Rainbow Bridge. Muffin, who I'm sure you've seen from her photographs, is very much a sort of 'mini-me' of Dexter, suddenly began sitting on Dexter's mat near the bird table, where Dexter spent many happy hours close to his feathered friends. It appeared to me and Juliet that perhaps little Muffin had decided to take over his 'job' of being the guardian of our daily avian visitors. She has carried on doing this for the two years since we lost Dexter, so if anyone can explain how this came to be, I'd really like to know.

RIP Dexter

Dexter's life story became an Amazon UK bestseller on the day of its release and became the first of my books to win three literary awards, a great tribute to the life of a truly unique, loving dog.

Dexter's Memorial Garden

Remembering Dexter, The Book

With our pack reduced to ten, life slowly returned to normal after the loss of our beautiful Dexter and it became obvious to Juliet and me that the previous ultra-close relationship between Muffin, Digby and Petal was gradually being 'invaded' by our latest addition. We'd always described owing the three puppies as being like having one dog with twelve legs, due to them doing everything together. Those three dogs literally stuck to each other like glue; what one did, the other two would join in. It certainly made finding them easy, just call one, and three would quickly arrive. Now though, we noticed a subtle change in the dynamic between the dogs. More and more, little Honey would force herself into the puppies' daily routines, in the house, in the garden and even on walks or playing time on the field.

During the day, Digby has always loved spending time in what we call his 'day bed' in the utility room, the other dogs have 7 beds to choose from in the kitchen while Penny and Cassie spend the daytime in the lounge and hallway. A lot of the time, Digby would be joined by Petal and Muffin in his day bed, and all three would snuggle together for a snooze. Now, however, we couldn't help noticing that little Honey had forced herself into the equation. Instead of Digby sharing his bed with his sisters, we would find, for example, Digby, Muffin and Honey, or perhaps Petal Muffin and Honey in his bed, with the odd one out having to find another bed somewhere else to relax in.

I had a thought and one day said to Juliet, "We've always thought of them as being like the three musketeers, Aramis, Porthos and Athos, but now, it looks like they'd been joined by their version of D'Artagnan." Honey had certainly made herself 'part of the gang' and the three pups accepted her as being 'one of them' and that's been the situation ever since.

Digby, Honey and Muffin

And on another day, it might be...

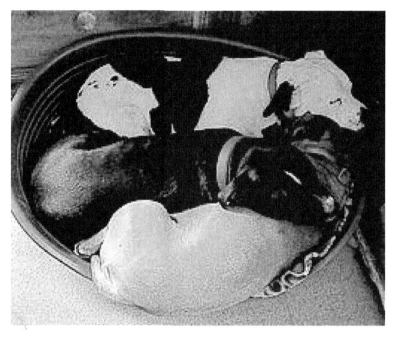

Petal Muffin and Honey

With Honey's arrival, the whole pack was revitalised and even the older dogs seemed to find a new lease of life, with Sheba managing to join in playtimes despite her arthritis. The oldest dogs, Penny, Cassie and Dylan also found their second wind, and even Muttley looked as though he wanted to act like a puppy all over again. Life was good and it was great for us to have such a happy band of dogs with which to share our lives.

13

THAT DARNED LEG AGAIN

IT WAS around the time when we said our last goodbyes to Dexter that Digby came home from his afternoon walk one day, limping quite badly. We could see straight away that the problem was in his right front leg. He clearly wasn't putting his full weight on it as he walked and because of his problems in earlier life we lost no time in making an appointment for him to see the vet, the very next day.

On arrival at the veterinary surgery, the reception staff made a big fuss of Digby, who they hadn't seen for some time, apart from his regular annual visits for his booster jabs. Digby of course lapped up the attention, and I could swear his limp suddenly got worse, or was he cleverly 'milking' his injury to obtain the maximum attention?

We didn't have to wait long to be seen and Ximo, (our Spanish vet, pronounced Cheemo) examined Digby's injured leg, and to be on the safe side, the other three as well. It didn't take long for him to announce that Digby's juvenile elbow dysplasia had reared its ugly head again. Ximo decided that the best course of action would be to introduce Digby to a regular daily dose of a joint supplement. He recommended we use YuMove, a well-known and highly effective supplement to help support Digby's joint ailment. He prescribed the tablets and we started Digby on them that day. He also gave him a pain killing injection and prescribed Metacam, to be used as a painkiller for the next ten days.

The final part of his instructions regarding Digby's treatment plan, however, was sure to prove the hardest part for Juliet and me to implement. When Ximo said to me, "Try and get him to rest his leg for about a week to ten days at least," I couldn't help laughing.

"You must be joking, Ximo," I replied. "Do you have any suggestions of how we tell Digby he's no allowed to run and play with his sisters, and even worse, with Honey?"

"You can restrict him to lead walks only until he's walking a bit better," Ximo said, hopefully.

"Oh yes, that's not a problem where walks are concerned, but the bigger problem will be curtailing his playtimes around the house and garden. It will be virtually impossible to watch him twenty-four hours a day to ensure he's not going mental in the garden with the other dogs or even playing in the house."

Ximo seemed to contemplate for long seconds before finally replying.

"Brian, I know it'll be difficult, but for Digby's sake, you'll just have to do the best you can."

Leaving the surgery soon afterwards, armed with a new bottle of Metacam, and having been given a follow-up appointment to take Digby for a check-up on the leg in two weeks' time, I arrived home and related the events at the surgery to Juliet, who like I had with Ximo, laughed when I told her the bit about making Digby rest his leg.

"Oh yes, that'll be right," she responded. "He's going to be bad enough being restricted to lead walks, and not being allowed to run around on the field, but we'll never be able to stop him joining in when they're playing in the garden."

"I know, but we'll just have to do our best to make sure he doesn't make it any worse," I said, as Digby sat at me feet, his tail wagging, knowing we were talking about him, without knowing just what we were discussing of course. If he'd known exactly what we were talking about, I doubt his tail would be wagging so happily, poor little fella.

Resting that pesky leg

Both Juliet and I were pleasantly surprised at how well

Digby reacted to being placed on 'restrictions' as it was as if he understood that we were doing our best to help him. Obviously, despite the painkillers, he must have still been suffering some pain in his leg which naturally would slow him down, but he even adjusted extremely well to being taken on lead walks instead of going for his usual daily runs with his doggie pals. His exceptional behaviour even extended to the home, where he seemed content to spend most of his time in the garden relaxing on one of the outdoor beds we provide for the dogs. Thankfully the weather was good at the time and like all the dogs, he enjoyed nothing better than lying out there, soaking up the sun, until he got too hot and would move indoors and carry on 'chilling' in his day bed in the utility room, or in one of the beds in the kitchen. Evenings were no problem at all, as the usual routine saw all the dogs being allowed in the lounge where they would spend the time with us. Digby, Muffin and Petal, (and latterly Honey), would all join Juliet on the sofa where they'd cuddle up with her, either on the sofa itself, or quite often one or more of them would stretch out across the back of the sofa.

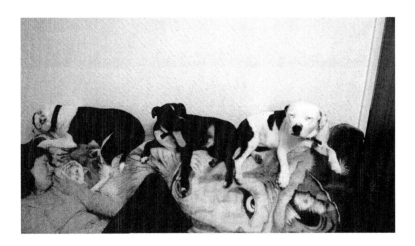

Meanwhile, I'd be in my armchair where I could relax in relative peace, usually being joined by Sasha, who would stretch out across my lap, where she'd fall asleep in seconds and would soon be gently snoring happily as I attempted to watch the TV. Sometimes her snoring would get a bit too loud and at such times the TV remote control became my best friend as I gradually increased the volume of the TV so I could hear whatever I was watching over and above the sound of Sasha's snoring. You might ask why I didn't try to stop her from snoring. The truth is, I loved having her with me on the chair and she just looked so happy and peaceful, curled up on my lap that I just didn't have the heart to disturb her.

Me and my girl

Time soon passed and it was time to take Digby back to the vet for his follow-up examination. Ximo wasn't entirely happy with Digby's progress. He decided to take x-rays of the offending joint and as a result of those, he came to the decision that Digby had a weakness in the joint and though not requiring surgery, he recommended that we keep Digby on the joint supplements on a permanent basis. He also recommended a series of steroid injections, one every month for three months, to help build up the joint. The injections did seem to help and Digby began to move more freely.

Consequently, Digby has been taking YuMove supplements ever since. Proof that they were helping him, combined with the injections, came within about three months, when we noticed the limp had completely gone. I took him to see Ximo once again and he was delighted to see how well Digby was walking. The daily supplements were clearly working as they were supposed to and Ximo simply told us to carry on with the YuMove, and he also gave me a large bottle of Metacam with instructions to put Digby on the painkiller for a week if he showed any sign of distress or if the limp suddenly reappeared. Thankfully, since that time, we've only had to use the Metacam on about four occasions, so it's safe to assume that Digby's joint problem is well and truly under control.

It might seem as if Digby is tending to hog the limelight a little in the puppies' story and I must confess that's probably true, not due to any favouritism of course, but simply because most of the problems that have affected the three dogs seem to have centred on poor old Digby. Apart from their own problems with elbow dysplasia when they were little more than puppies, Petal and Muffin have remained virtually 100% fit and healthy, apart from the occasional minor flare up of that old problem, though never serious enough to require further veterinary treatment.

When I think about how rough Honey is when she plays with them, I have to think they must be blessed in some way, never to have suffered a single serious injury or illness between them, apart from one incident involving little Muffin.

105

During the last year that Victoria was living at home with us, during her regular Saturday grooming session, Juliet called my attention to the fact that one of Muffin's teats appeared to have grown larger all of a sudden. At first, we wondered if she might have caught it on something sharp while she'd been out on one of her walks. Walking in the woods every day exposed the dogs to all sorts of potential hazards, with spiky bramble bushes and other dangerous (for dogs) plants lying in wait for an unwary pup.

We decided to keep an eye on the overgrown nipple for the next few days to see if the swelling reduced. Unfortunately, instead of shrinking, the teat continued to grow larger, and we decided that it would be prudent to book Muffin in for an appointment with the vet. By the time Muffin and I arrived for her appointment, the nipple had grown considerably bigger, and Juliet and I were worried in case it was a symptom of something serious.

Muffin was seen by the other Spanish vet at our Surgery, Carolina, who gave our little girl a thorough examination. She told me it was most probably a benign swelling of the teat but that to be on the safe side and to ensure it wasn't cancerous, she would take a sample from the teat and perform a biopsy. The result of the biopsy was reassuring. There was no sign of cancer, but Carolina advised me that it would be best to remove the nipple to eliminate the threat of possible cancer in the future, and I immediately booked Muffin in for the operation.

A week later, I arrived at the surgery just after 8am and we were booked in and only had a short wait before being called through to a consultation room. The nurse went through the usual booking-in procedure, and I signed the necessary consent form and then came the moment when I had to leave Muffin with her. The look on poor Muffin's face when she realised I was going without her! She looked so bereft, and her tail drooped down between her legs. The nurse did her best to reassure her, cuddling her and talking softly to her, but Muffin was so upset and panicky. I had no choice but to turn my back and quickly left the room, feeling so guilty for leaving her, but knowing it was for her own good.

Just after 2pm I received a call from Carolina to inform me that Muffin had been operated on and had just woken up a while ago. She was pleased to report that Muffin was perfectly ok, and I could collect her at 5pm. When I picked her up later that day, she virtually dragged the poor nurse through the door when she brought her out and she saw me. She was still a bit 'groggy' from the effects of the anaesthetic but that didn't stop her showing how happy she was to see me. Her tail began wagging furiously and she couldn't wait to go home.

That face!

When we did arrive home, her brother and sister, who'd visibly been missing her through the day, were almost ecstatic to see her again, as was little Honey. We had to make sure they didn't get too rough with their greetings as we couldn't risk them disturbing her stitches. Her medical notes carried the warning about the stitches problem, and we were pleased to see they'd used the correct ones on Muffin this time. Strangely enough, after they'd all had a sniff round her, (she clearly had that special 'vet' scent about her), they calmed down and mostly left her alone. Perhaps they could sense she was still affected by the anaesthetic, because poor Muffin was definitely a bit dopey for the rest of the evening, though she was hungry enough to eat everything in her bowl that evening.

She was limited to lead walks for a few days, until she'd been back to the vets for a check-up, which severely limited her playful nature, but the time soon passed with Muffin showing no signs that the operation had upset her in any way at all. At her post-operative check-up five days later, I was delighted when Muffin was declared fit and well, and ready to resume normal walks. Very soon, our 'four musketeers' were once again zooming around on the playing field, with their games of rough and tumble once again back on the agenda.

Home from her operation, flaked out!

14

GOODBYE TO SASHA

Treat time for Muttley, Sheba, Digby, Petal, Sasha, and
slightly hidden, Dexter and Muffin

I'VE OPENED this chapter with what I've always felt was such a beautiful picture of the 'Staffy brigade' obediently queueing for treats, at a time before we lost poor Dexter and Sasha. You can see from the background that it was long before I created Dexter's Memorial Garden, but it shows how well-behaved the gang were, even with food about.

I know people, especially some of our friends, who have maybe two or three dogs and they tell us it can be a nightmare trying to hand treats out to their dogs due to the potential fall-outs between their greedy pups, hands being nipped or worse, and general mayhem in behavioural terms. Is it a case of poor training, or just that they have unruly dogs that can't be controlled? I don't have any answers for that but can only say that we've never had a problem with the behaviour of our dogs when it's time for handing out the treats.

Mum handing out bits of bacon

Meanwhile time was passing, and before we knew it our beautiful puppies were celebrating their seventh birthdays. Honey was two years old already and before long, our gorgeous girl, Sasha, the undoubted leader of the pack would be celebrating her tenth birthday, or so we thought. None of us could envisage the disaster that was about to befall our family.

One beautiful, warm and sunny summer's day in July 2020, the dogs were enjoying lying out in the back garden, soaking up the sun. It was a perfect summer's scene, one that had been repeated many times over the years, our dogs at peace, snoozing in the warmth of a summer's day.

That was, until I walked outside into the garden after having eaten my lunch. I could tell straight away, just by looking at her, that there was something wrong with Sasha. This was not an epileptic seizure. She'd had enough of those over the years, and both Juliet and I could instantly recognise the symptoms of such a fit, but this was different. I won't describe the details, as it would be too upsetting to relate, but I think both Juliet and I knew straight away that our 'baby girl' had suffered a stroke!

Together, we gently picked Sasha up and equally gently laid her in the back of the car. I phoned the vet and told them we were coming, and why. We knew what had to be done, but Juliet hadn't said a word. She knew Sasha was 'my dog' and she'd left it to me to make that final decision. At the vets surgery, the staff were waiting as we pulled up in the car, and though two of the nurses were ready with a stretcher, Carl, a male receptionist, insisted on picking Sasha up and lovingly carried her into the surgery and into a consulting room. What happened next was too upsetting to relate in detail, but I was able to spend some time saying my final goodbyes to my beautiful Sasha, before the vet, together with a nurse took great care in sending my little girl on her journey across the Rainbow

Bridge. I was left alone with her for about fifteen minutes, as I cried and cried for my Sasha. All I could think of was that at least she wouldn't have to suffer any more seizures, but somehow that didn't make up for losing my very best friend.

The hurt of Sasha's loss was immense. She'd been by my side, non-stop for over nine years and now, she was gone, just like that. Whenever I got up to go from room to room, Sasha would follow me, when I went upstairs for a bath, Sasha would follow me and sit beside the bath, guarding me; she was my shadow. She even knew somehow, when I was about to suffer an angina attack and had a way of warning me, so that I had time to sit or lie down before the attack began. She then stayed with me and wouldn't let me move until I was fully recovered. She truly was an amazing, empathic little dog.

In the days following her death, and after I'd announced it on Facebook, where she had so many fans and followers, we received cards, flowers, gifts and over 2,000 messages of condolence, surely a mark of the love that people felt for my baby girl all around the world. As I sit writing this chapter, it's just over a week away from the first anniversary of her passing. I know for sure that we'll shed a few tears on that day, as we remember our special, very precious Sasha.

Me and my girl

With the loss of Sasha, our canine family was reduced to nine dogs. Some people may think that's a lot of dogs to handle, but quite honestly, our house really felt empty for the first few weeks without her.

But life has to go on and so it did as we continued to enjoy our time with the rest of our wonderful pack. Of course, there was hardly a moment's peace with the 'four musketeers' around. Muffin, Digby and Petal, with their sidekick, Honey, certainly made sure of that.

One day, after returning from his afternoon walk with Juliet and Honey, we noticed that Digby's eye appeared to be swollen and bleeding. On investigation we found a small cyst in the corner of his eye, that he must have caught on something during his walk, unless Honey had managed to scratch it with her claws while they were playing on the field. We didn't want to take any chances with it being his eye that was affected and so once again, I took Digby to see the vet. Thankfully, Carolina confirmed that it was just a harmless cyst, and she gave us some cream to apply to the affected area which would help the swelling go down. Juliet couldn't help commenting, "Why is it always Digby? The others never seem to be affected by such things. It's always him."

There was no way I could give her anything like a truthful answer. None of us knew why Digby seemed to be the one who was always in the wars. But at least the cyst wasn't causing him any pain, or affecting his sight, so in fact on this occasion, he'd got off lightly.

I'm sure the other dogs missed Sasha, especially the three pups she'd raised from a few weeks old, and of course, Honey, who she'd not only been a second mum to, but an almost constant playmate. They must have wondered where she was, particularly as she was without doubt, the leader of the pack. None of the dogs however, missed her as much as Sheba. Despite being some years older than Sasha, Sheba had come to depend on Sasha, in many ways. Remembering that Sheba had suffered a terrible start in life, being used as a bait dog by dog fighters, we realised that she had come to look upon Sasha as her 'protector' and she'd spend a lot of time with Sasha, either playing with her, or just as 'someone' to cuddle up with.

Sheba and Sasha Best Friends Forever

As she'd grown older, Sheba had developed some mobility problems and eventually she was diagnosed with osteoarthritis. Caroline the vet prescribed joint supplements and painkillers for her, and for a while she seemed to cope quite well. One day, in the summer of 2000, Juliet and I became especially worried about her, when we found her lying on her side in the utility room and it was soon obvious to both of us that Sheba was unable to get up onto her own four legs. She was struggling and we feared the worst. If her legs had failed her, it looked very much as if I was facing another heart-rending trip to the vet. We both agonised over whether or not to make that fateful decision and just as I was about to pick up the phone to tell the vet I was coming on a sad journey, Sheba confounded us by somehow struggling up until she was standing proudly on all four legs, her tail wagging as if to tell us it wasn't time for her to leave us yet.

Over the next two weeks we monitored her closely. She couldn't walk very well, but she was determined to try. I did in fact take her to the vet, who prescribed a course of painkillers which seemed to help her temporarily. Then one day, I saw an advertisement on the internet. A company was advertising their 'Joint Chews', which were supposedly almost miraculous in their effects on dogs with severe joint problems. I looked up the reviews and they certainly had some terrific testimonials, so I said to Juliet,

"If these are as good as the reviews make them out to be, they could make a big difference to Sheba. I'm going to order some and try them."

Juliet agreed with my decision, and I placed an order. It was the best thing I'd ever done for Sheba. Within days of her beginning to take the Pet Lab Joint Chews, we saw a difference in her walking ability. The little bone-shaped, pork-flavoured chews transformed our crippled old girl's life. She was still quite wobbly when she walked, but the important thing was, she appeared to be pain-free, and when we saw her trying to play with Honey, we knew we'd done the right thing in ordering the chews. They're not cheap, but they definitely do what the company said they'd do. Sheba still couldn't go out for real walks, but she was happy toddling around the house and garden. She's been taking one a day every since then.

One day, Juliet met a lady while out walking Honey and Petal, who out of the blue asked Juliet if we could make use of a dog stroller, as her old dog had sadly died and she had no use for it any longer. Of course, it would be great for Sheba, so Juliet arranged to collect it from the lady's home and once again, Sheba's quality of life was improved greatly. She loved being taken for 'walks' in her stroller, as we went around the village with Sheba having a great view of everything and the stroller proved quite a talking point as people would come up to us and make a fuss of her and ask how old she was etc.

Happy Sheba in her stroller

Such was the success of the Pet Lab Joint Chews, that after a few months of Sheba taking her one a day, she was walking so much better, and she was making such a fuss when I was getting ready to take the dogs for walks, that I decided to try taking her for a short walk, around the block to see how she coped with a return to 'walkies'.

She absolutely loved it. It was just a short, ten-minute walk, with blind Dylan walking slowly beside her, but Sheba was so happy to be out and about, under her own power once again. Going by the success of that short excursion I began taking her out for similar short walks twice a week at first, and now, after nearly a year on the chews, she's walking with me and Dylan every other day. It's slow, sometimes she staggers a little, and once or twice, she's fallen over when she's lost her balance, but 99% of the time, she completes her walks with a big 'staffy smile' on her face.

I'll close this chapter with a last goodbye to Sasha, who without a doubt played a massive part in the lives of Muffin, Digby and Petal especially, as well as Honey and every dog that became a part of 'her' pack. She really was a very special dog.

Recently, Next Chapter Publishing have released a new 3rd edition of Sasha's life story which details the final years of her wonderful life, up to her tragic death in 2020. Sasha will always be with us, in our wonderful memories of her, in our minds and in our thoughts. She most definitely left her pawprints on our hearts.

15

FEATHERS AND FUNNY FACES

BACK TO THE main story now, and time to focus on that boy again. Yes, Digby is once again the subject of the narrative, this time for a look at the funny side of our beautiful young fella. As I'm sure most of you who are reading this book are aware, Staffordshire Bull Terriers have acquired something of an undeserved reputation over the years, of being nasty, rough, tough dogs. Though that description probably applies to a certain minority of the breed, I'd definitely say such cases are almost invariably caused by poor training, or simply by owners who callously train their dogs to be vicious, in other words, they weaponise their innocent dogs in order to turn them into attack dogs. This isn't something that applies only to staffies, as almost any breed can be trained to be vicious by the wrong kind of owner.

I can honestly say that over the years, we have only known love, affection and faithfulness from the staffies we've owned. Digby and his sisters are of course only half staffy, the other half being Springer Spaniel. I say this to help illustrate a partic-ular trait of Digby's. Ever since he was a young pup, Digby has been afraid of...feathers! Yes, that's what I said, he's scared to death of bird feathers, even the tiniest examples, such as the little white fluffy ones you often find lying on the ground. With the vast number of birds that visit our garden every day, you can imagine we get quite a number of little feathers lying around, quite frequently.

It's so funny to watch him, and the first time we noticed it we couldn't work out what on earth he was doing. It was obvious he was staring at something, and he appeared to be stalking whatever it was that had attracted his attention. Could it have been a fly? An ant perhaps? But flies and ants move around, don't they? Whatever he was stalking was obviously not moving, as he just stood there, staring down at the object of interest.

I very slowly walked towards him and when I saw the tiny feather on the ground in front of him, it was all I could do to stop myself breaking out in laughter. Juliet was watching me through the kitchen window, and I beckoned her to come out and look at the cause of Digby's paralysing fear. He was literally rooted to the spot as if he was afraid to move. Juliet couldn't help herself; she really did burst out laughing.

"Digby, you big wuss," she laughed. "Don't tell me you're scared of a little tiny feather."

But of course, he was. He was 'rescued' from the vile, terribly threatening feather when Muffin trotted up to see what was going on. She took one look at this ultra-dangerous object that had instilled such paralysing fear in her brother...and promptly bent down, picked it up and swallowed it.

Feather alert!

As he's grown older, Digby has become a bit braver, in as much as occasionally, he will actually 'challenge' one of these terrible vicious beastly feathers by pawing at it, and if it doesn't instantly leap up and attack him, he will do as Muffin had demonstrated to him, and grab it and devour it, but only if it's very small and not likely to be too dangerous. Of course, now and then the feather will be caught by a slight breeze and be blown either into the air or along the ground, and if that should happen, you should see Digby run!

Get that feather Digby!

The strange thing about Digby's feather fixation is that it only apples to those little, down-like feathers you often see on the ground, but not to full-size wing or tail feathers. He will quite happily walk past a three or four inch, or even longer feather, but those tiny ones, no way. They're obviously severely dangerous, at least in Digby's mind. At least we know he's guaranteed to give us a good laugh from time to time as he fights his ongoing war against the evil invasion of the feathers.

Now, let's talk about faces. I don't mean the ordinary, everyday faces we all know and love our dogs for. Two of the puppies, Digby and Muffin, are also known to occasionally pull some really funny faces. They're dogs of course so I don't suppose they purposely decide to 'pull a face' just to amuse us, but when they do, it's guaranteed to bring a smile to our faces. Digby was actually still very young when he amused us with the following picture. I still wonder to this day what he was trying to say with this look. Though he might look as if he's asleep, I can honestly say he wasn't as Juliet said, "What a face Digby," and he instantly reacted by looking at her and wagging his tail, as if he was saying, "Who are you calling funny face?"

His features then returned to normal and we could only laugh at the strange, twisted face he'd pulled, which we thought made him look as if he was sucking a lemon. In the course of the years he's been with us, Digby has pulled many funny faces, but as most dog owners will know, they nearly always do things like this when you don't necessarily have a camera close to hand and the majority of those strange but funny faces just go unrecorded and forgotten about in time.

Funny face Digby

This next photo however is one of my favourites. I'm just glad I had my phone with me when he pulled this amazing face, which resembles a cross between a yawn and a canine impression of 'Jaws' the great white shark of movie fame. See what you think.

'Jaws'

Muffin also has the ability to amuse us with a few funny faces of her own, but like Digby, she tends to produce them when we're without a camera or a phone in our hand. I've been fortunate to have managed to get a couple of good pictures of her, usually when she's been in her 'talking' mode as I mentioned earlier in the book. The first of these pictures captured her in 'mid – sentence' as she tried to explain something to us. We've never yet managed to work out what she was saying of course, but it was so funny listening to her chattering away at us.

Chatterbox Muffin.

Most of her other funny faces tend to mirror her behaviour. She really knows how to 'put on' a guilty look, one most doggie folks will be aware of, you know, the one that says, "I know I shouldn't have done it, but I'm sorry, honest I am."

"I'm sorry, I didn't mean it."

Then of course there's the look that nobody can mistake for anything other than Muffin's cheeky face. This is the look we get when she's in playful mood, or when she's just about to do something she knows she shouldn't be doing but thinks that this look will excuse anything. After all, this is cheeky Muffin!

Cheeky Muffin

You might be asking where Petal is in this little rogues' gallery. That's a good question and the answer is quite simply that she doesn't appear in this collection of funny faces for the simple reason that Petal just doesn't pull funny faces. She virtually always has a very serious look on her face, and you have to know her to be able to work out just how her facial features tell us anything about how she's feeling. Perhaps her most telling look is her quizzical face, when she's unsure about a particular noise or something Juliet or I say to her. In such cases there's no mistaking the look that says, "What?"

"What are you telling me?"

That head on the side look is something she's done since she was a puppy as you can see from this early photo of her doing the same thing,

A confused puppy?

So, as you can see, poor Petal doesn't have much of a range of different facial expressions and even the picture that follows is just another way of Petal showing she's unsure about something.

"You talking to me?"

While writing this section, I've realised that perhaps I've done Petal an injustice. It would seem that, although not exactly 'funny' faces, she has provided us with some amusement as a result of some of the facial expressions I've captured on film over the years. If I tickle Petal just under her 'armpit' she does what in other dogs would probably be called a smile. In Petal's case it looks like a snarl, but I guarantee this is her version of a doggie smile! She loves it and encourages me to keep doing it, so that says it all really.

The Petal 'smile'

I thought I'd end this chapter with a little gallery featuring all three pups. You've already seen the picture that was used for the cover of this book, but what is rather unusual is that over the years, Muffin, Digby and Petal have taken many opportunities to gather together for similar group photographs. They seem to relish the chance to get together for a group photo as you'll see from the following collection. I think these pictures just go to show how 'together' the three of them are.

It's probably worth mentioning that at the time we adopted them, more than one person warned us that we were asking for trouble in taking on three pups from the same litter, saying that they were bound to fall out, perhaps fighting and doing some serious harm to one or more of the trio.

"It never works," somebody told us, and "You're just asking for trouble," said another. Well, here we are, about to celebrate the pups' ninth birthday, and we're still waiting for the first sign of any trouble or falling out between them.

So, here we go with the trio collection.

A few weeks old

4 years old

Three 'bruisers'

Still the same, 2021

Sleepy puppies

Garden sunshine

Evening relaxation

16

DOGS AND DENTISTRY

I'VE ALREADY MENTIONED that it seems the years have flown since we brought the three puppies home for the first time. So much has happened, though much of the events that have transpired didn't directly impact on the trio. Muffin, Digby and Petal have always been the happiest of dogs, with nothing appearing to upset them, either singly or collectively.

After an almost perfect upbringing, guided by Juliet and me, and aided by Sasha's canine guidance, they really have been an absolute joy to have as parts of our family. No matter their ages, they've continued to reinforce our belief that they really are like 'one dog with twelve legs', happily going through life together as a single entity, or so it appears.

Bedtime with Sasha

I'm including a couple more photos of them with Sasha in this chapter, because as I sit writing it, it happens to be a year this week since we lost our beautiful girl and I know the dogs have all missed her in their own way. Petal in particular has made Sasha's bed in our bedroom her own, and when we go up to bed, she always first into the bedroom where she quickly curls up on the bed and will only grudgingly allow Muffin to join her later in the night. To begin with, Muffin is banished to one of the other beds in the room. Digby of course has his own bed on Juliet's side of the bed.

Petal and Sasha

Playtimes for the three pups, and Honey of course tend to be as lively and as raucous as ever. Honey now loves it when Petal and Muffin play rough with her. Anyone seeing Petal and Muffin pinning Honey to the ground on her back and 'ragging' her around in the garden would, I'm sure, think they were pulling her to pieces, when in fact all three are having a great time play-fighting with nobody getting so much as a scratch despite the sight and the sounds they make while wrestling around as if their lives depend on the outcome.

Playtime

Petal and Muffin

I'd love to include a photo of them all, including Honey, playing together but as most dog owners will know, dogs can be so uncooperative sometimes, and though I have a couple of videos of them all having fun together, every time I've tried to get a still photo of them at play, they stop as soon as they realise I'm pointing the phone camera at them and all I have are a couple of out-of-focus efforts which are certainly not good enough to include in this story.

Soon after Sasha left us for the Rainbow Bridge, we were concerned when we discovered a large swelling on Muttley's jaw. Fearing the worst, I arranged a vet appointment and was relieved when an examination, followed by a biopsy showed he had a large, benign tumour growing on his lower jaw. The bad news was that it had grown around one of his incisors, so they would need to operate to remove the growth and the tooth, as the gum had become infected. He was booked in for his operation a week later and good old Muttley, who by then was nearly 11 years old, was the perfect patient, both at the vets and when he came home. In fact, he was so good, we hardly knew he'd undergone the operation.

Muttley relaxing after his operation

Muttley received a clean bill of health a week later at his post-operative check-up and soon returned to his normal walks and his favourite pastime, sunbathing! Muttley loves nothing more than sitting in the sunshine and takes every opportunity to 'top up his tan' and of course he really loves his twice-daily walks with me.

No sooner had Muttley recovered from his operation, we noticed that our pack's 'elder-statesman' Dylan, who was nearing sixteen years of age, seemed to be having trouble eating his daily meals. He was as enthusiastic as always at feeding times, but for some reason he was leaving quite a lot of his food. Dylan had been gradually losing both his hearing and his sight and had survived two mini-strokes a couple of years earlier, and we were fearful that it might be time to let him follow Sasha and Dexter to the Rainbow Bridge. A visit to the vet soon sorted out the problem. Dylan's teeth had never been very good, due to the abuse he'd suffered in his early life and now, Carolina informed me, his gums had become infected, and it was obviously causing the pain when he tried to eat. The only solution was to have Dylan's teeth removed.

"What? All of them?" I asked, feeling shocked at the thought of our little boy without any teeth.

"We might be able to leave him a couple of teeth but won't know which ones or how many until we get him under the anaesthetic," she informed me.

We didn't really have a choice and so I agreed to the operation and a few days later, I returned to the surgery with Dylan, and I admit, I was quite worried, leaving our little old man behind when I went home after dropping him off. I needn't have worried. I received a phone call from one of the veterinary nurses soon after lunchtime to say that Dylan had had his operation and was awake and doing well. I could collect him around five o'clock, and when I arrived at the surgery, I was told that Dylan had been their star patient of the day. Everyone had wanted to give him cuddles and he'd received so much love from all the staff, probably because of his age and his sight and hearing problems. When the nurse brought him out to me, he walked with a spring in his step, and I was told he'd eaten a meal of soft dog meat without any trouble. It made me feel guilty that he'd clearly been in pain for some time with the infected gums, and I'd failed to notice the problem, but the nurse reassured me that dogs are very good at hiding things from us, which we knew, and that it wasn't our fault.

The good news was that Carolina had been able to save a few of his teeth so he still had something to crunch small biscuits with. We were amazed at the change in Dylan who suddenly seemed to gain a new lease of life. He ate all his meals, just soft meat now, though he did enjoy the little 'puppy bones' treats I bought him from the pet shop.

Dylan and Juliet

He showed an extra spring in his step during our walks, and it was obvious that having his teeth removed was the best thing we could have done for him. A year later, and Dylan's still going strong as he approaches his seventeenth birthday.

Soon after Dylan's dental problem was solved, another incident arose that made us think we were suffering from a curse of dental issues. Just when everything was going well, and all the dogs seemed happy and healthy, Juliet noticed that Digby appeared to be having a problem eating his evening meal. She allowed him to finish his tea, which took him longer than usual and then she decided to take a look in his mouth.

"Brian, you'd better take a look at this," she called me from where I was supervising the dogs who have their tea in the kitchen. Muffin, Digby, Petal and Honey are fed in the utility room, Sheba and Muttley in the kitchen, Cassie in the lounge, Penny in the hallway and Dylan outside in the fresh air.

"What's wrong?" I asked and she made Digby sit as she opened his mouth to show me what she'd discovered.

As she held his jaws open, I saw straight away what she was indicating to me. I groaned with the realisation that we had a third dog with a dental problem.

"Oh no, not you too, Diggers," I said to him as I stroked his head softly.

Digby had an obvious growth on his gum, positioned on or near to one his rear molars. It looked quite red and sore and certainly explained why he was having difficulty eating or swallowing his food.

"I'd better make him an appointment to see Carolina," I told Juliet, who agreed her special boy needed to be seen as soon as possible.

Next morning, I phoned the surgery and made an appointment for Digby to be seen later that day. At the allotted time we arrived at the vet's surgery and Digby received lots of love and cuddles from the staff in reception. He's such a lovable dog that everyone just had to come and have a moment with him. When it was our turn to be seen, Carolina examined his mouth very carefully and confirmed that he had an abscess on his gum which was growing over his tooth. The tooth itself would need to be extracted and the abscess removed, and his operation was scheduled for the following week. Carolina reassured me that it was a fairly routine operation, and that Digby would be able to return home later the same day.

A week later, I dropped Digby off soon after eight o'clock in the morning, after going through the usual admittance procedure, consent for anaesthetic etc. I went home, leaving our little boy looking rather bereft at me abandoning him, but the nurse distracted him from seeing me go by giving him lots of love and cuddles. Have I told you before, what a wimp poor Digby can be?

Back home, and the other dogs, especially Muffin and Petal soon realised Digby wasn't with me and his sisters seemed agitated throughout the morning, clearly missing their brother. When the phone rang soon after two pm that afternoon, I could see it was the vet calling so expected to be told that everything had gone well and that I could pick him up at teatime. It wasn't quite that simple, however.

"Mr Porter," Carolina said, with a hint of uneasiness in her voice, "I have some bad news, I'm afraid."

I instantly thought she was about to tell me that Digby had died while under the anaesthetic or something equally tragic.

"Oh, no, Carolina. What's wrong?"

"Digby has had his operation, and all went well. He's come round from the anaesthetic and should be ready to go home in a couple of hours. However, while he was under the anaesthetic, I took the time to do a thorough examination and I'm afraid I've found something unsettling. A scan revealed a growth on his spleen, and we've confirmed it with ultrasound. It looks as if Digby has a tumour."

"There it was," she'd said it, and I had a good idea where this was leading.

"Are we talking cancer?" I asked.

"It looks like it," she replied.

"Oh no, poor little Digby," I replied, shocked at the thought. "What can we do for him?"

"I'd like to send him for a scan at the veterinary hospital in Wakefield. They'll confirm the diagnosis and an appropriate course of action. In all likelihood any treatment will probably include the removal of his spleen."

"But tell me straight, please Carolina, if it's confirmed as cancer, can it be treated?"

"That will be up to the oncologist in Wakefield. They'll want to see him and conduct an examination, before they can decide on a course of treatment,"

I was virtually speechless at this news, and it was all I could do to arrange with Carolina for me to collect Digby at 5 pm that afternoon, at which time she'd tell me more. It was only after I'd hung up that I remembered Juliet was standing behind me, listening in, as I'd got my speakerphone turned on. She'd heard everything!

"Oh God," she exclaimed as I hung up and turned round to see the worry instantly etched across her face. This was her special boy, Digby we were talking about, and neither of us could ignore the fact that Carolina had mentioned the dreaded word 'cancer'.

"He can't have cancer, he only went in to have a tooth out, for God's sake."

All I could do initially was put my arms around her, give her a big hug, and try to reassure her that nothing was confirmed yet and that we'd do everything we possibly could to help our gorgeous little boy.

"You heard what Carolina said, she'll refer him to the specialists at the veterinary hospital and they'll be the best people to tell us what the various treatments are, if they apply to Digby's case. The first thing to do is bring him home this afternoon and let him recover fully from today's operation. In a way, we're lucky that Carolina did the full examination while he was knocked out. At least she's found it and we can get him the necessary treatment. If he hadn't had that op today, we'd never have known about this damn tumour, and it would have carried on growing inside him."

Poor Juliet visibly shuddered at the thought.

"Let's not get worked up too much until we know for certain there's something to worry about," I tried to reassure her.

The next couple of hours seemed to drag as we waited for the time for me to go and collect Digby. Finally, I was able to drive the few miles to the vets to collect our boy. Digby was of course ecstatic when he saw me and his tail wagged furiously and he jumped up, his front paws on my legs as he greeted me. After the initial greeting, Carolina explained in more detail what she'd told me on the phone.

"While I had him under the anaesthetic, I thought it would be a good time to give him a thorough examination and check-up. I felt something when I was checking the relevant area and decided to do an ultrasound scan which confirmed my initial thoughts. Digby definitely has quite a big mass in the area of his spleen, and he definitely needs treatment."

Of course, I was full of questions and Carolina was great, patiently answering all my queries. She explained that the hospital in Wakefield had every facility on-site and would give Digby the best treatment possible. The first step was to let him fully recover from his dental procedure, after which he could be seen by the oncologist. I needed to take Digby back to the surgery in three days for a post-op check, and if all was well, Carolina would then make the referral to the hospital and things could move forward from that point.

Digby takes it easy

Digby was more than pleased to see his Mum again when we arrived home, and if I'd thought he was excited to see me when I went to pick him up, that was nothing compared to the greeting he gave Juliet. His tail wagged at about a hundred miles an hour, his whole rear end wagging with it. He ran around in circles, jumped up at his Mum and gave her lots of wet sloppy kisses. Juliet wanted to hug him but had to wait a few minutes until he'd calmed down enough to be able to do so. We'd arrived home just in time for the dogs' feeding time and we wondered if he'd be interested in eating after the procedure in his mouth. We needn't have worried. Juliet put his tea out with all the others, and he devoured it as if he hadn't been fed for a week.

The next couple of days seemed to fly past, and Juliet made sure she gave her special little boy lots of extra love and cuddles, in fact we both did. I took Digby for his post-op check-up as scheduled and Carolina was happy that he'd recovered well from the surgery on his mouth, and she agreed that the next thing to do was for her to make the official referral to the veterinary hospital, which I now learned was known as Paragon

Referrals. The next thing I'd hear, she informed me, would be a call from Paragon to book Digby in for an initial appointment.

Time now appeared to stand still for Juliet and me as we waited for the fateful call that would set Digby on the way towards obtaining the necessary treatment for that horrible growth inside his little body. For now, though, all we could do was wait.

17

PARAGON REFERRALS

A WEEK after attending the surgery with Digby for his post-op check-up I received the call we'd been waiting for. A receptionist from Paragon Referrals called to offer me an appointment with Rodney Ayl, the oncologist, the following week.

As I had no idea how to get to the hospital, they agreed to send me a map and written instructions on how to get to them. As they handle referrals from all over the country, I presumed this was pretty much a standard procedure for them. Wakefield is only about 25 miles from where we live, as the crow flies, but getting there by road was a different matter. Studying the map, I saw that I would have to travel on three different motorways before negotiating my way through the roads and streets of Wakefield to get to the hospital, in a massive dogleg of a journey. The following day, I received a phone call from Rodney, explaining what would happen when I attended the appointment.

I would need to leave Digby with them for the day, and he'd be given an anaesthetic, after which Rodney would carry out the exploratory procedure, opening him up so he could carry out a full examination of the mass, as he referred to the growth on Digby's spleen and also to do whatever scans he felt necessary. Rodney was really good and asked if I had any questions. I said to him, "Rodney, I've probably got a hundred questions I want to ask, but for the moment they've gone right out of my head." He laughed, "I understand, just try not to worry. If you think of anything you want to know between now and the day of his appointment, just give us a call and we'll try to answer your queries."

I thanked him and asked what Juliet and I had decided was the most important question of all.

"Rodney, please tell me honestly what Digby's chances are if it's confirmed as cancer?"

"Okay," he replied. "First of all, I need to tell you that the majority of masses such as the one showing on the scan from your vet usually turn out to be non-cancerous, and that's what we need to hope for in Digby's case. If it does turn out to be a cancerous growth, then we have various options open to us, but those are best discussed once the diagnosis is confirmed."

That was really all we needed to know at that point, so I thanked Rodney and hung up. I knew that Juliet and I weren't going to be able to relax or even sleep properly till we knew just what was wrong with Digby and just what that growth inside him really was. Was it cancer? Was it a benign growth? Would our little fella be okay? How long could we expect to have him if the worst-case scenario showed up during his examination?

As that week slowly ticked by, we gave Digby lots of love and cuddles as usual, but I could see just how worried Juliet was getting the closer we got to the day of his examination. We were up extremely early on the day of his appointment in Wakefield. We'd barely slept the night before. They say that dogs have a marvellous intuition as to when something is about to happen, and that night before his exploratory operation, Digby actually changed his sleeping habits.

When we went upstairs to bed, with the three pups having preceded us upstairs as usual, we were surprised to find Digby on our bed, having made himself comfortable on Juliet's side of the bed.

Cheeky boy!

"Excuse me," Juliet exclaimed with amusement. "Who said you could get up on our bed, you cheeky boy?"

By way of a reply, Digby looked pleadingly at Juliet, while his tail beat a steady rhythm on the bed as if to say, "I know you don't mind, really, Mum."

Of course, we couldn't be angry with him. We felt sure he knew something unusual was about to happen and he wanted some extra love and cuddles, which Juliet provided him with in no small amount.

After spending a couple of minutes giving him the required amount of affection, Juliet made him get down and told him to go in his own bed. Digby reluctantly gave up his place on our bed, jumped down and appeared to have settled down in his own bed, positioned right next to Juliet's side of the bed. Before we finally put the lights out and settled down for the night, we looked to make sure all three dogs were curled up in their beds, and I was surprised when Juliet said to me, "Digby's not in his bed."

Quickly looking round the room, I found Digby had decided he wanted some doggy company, and he was comfortably snuggled up in bed with little Muffin. He must have stayed there for most of the night, but when we woke in the morning he was back in his own bed, close to his Mum. Did he know what was going to happen the next day? Was his doggy intuition at work and making him seek the close comfort and company of his sister? We'll never know, but it was the first time we could ever remember him doing this since he was a very young puppy.

Night before the exploratory operation

Due to him being scheduled for surgery, we were unable to give Digby any breakfast so he must have wondered what was going on. I'd estimated that the journey would take me about an hour, so Juliet took him for a short walk before I left home. She helped me load him into the back of the car and gave him a big hug and a cuddle before she dropped the tailgate and I set off on a journey none of us expected or wanted to be making just a couple of weeks ago. It was a very cold February morning as I headed towards the motorway on the first leg of the journey.

It was raining heavily, and the road surface was slippery, so I had to keep the speed down. I'd printed out a route map for my journey I'd found on Google Maps, and it sat on the passenger seat next to the written directions provided by Paragon as I kept my eyes peeled on the treacherous road surface, made worse by the spray thrown up by the numerous lorries and vans on the motorway at that early hour of day. I soon reached the interchange that took me from the M18 onto the M62 and felt better, knowing that we were gradually getting nearer our destination. Before I knew it, I changed once again, this time onto the M1, for just a few miles, after which I left the motorway system and found myself on a dual carriageway, heading towards the city of Wakefield, and thankfully the rain had stopped, which is where things began to go wrong.

Somehow, the printed directions I had on the seat next to me didn't seem to match up with the actual road layout as I drove in search of the various junctions and streets that would take me to Paragon Referrals. I certainly knew I'd gone wrong when I found myself on the entrance road to the massive Pinderfields Hospital. Knowing I must have missed a turning somewhere along my route, I pulled over and rang Paragon, where a helpful receptionist attempted to give me directions from where I was, to where I needed to be, though the young woman I spoke to admitted she wasn't from Wakefield herself and her directions could be wrong!

They *were* wrong, and a few minutes later I stopped once more and made another phone call. This time, the lady I spoke to informed me that the place I'd reached was only two minutes from my destination, gave me a couple of quick directions and before I knew it, we turned a corner and there, right in front of us, was Paragon. We'd made it with a couple of minutes to spare.

Seeing Paragon Referrals for the first time almost took my breath away. I was expecting something that looked like a regular veterinary surgery, perhaps a bit bigger. Instead, I was faced with an ultra-modern building with a plate glass and steel façade that was, quite frankly, massive. A beautiful reception area fronted the building which stretched away to the side and rear, making it the most impressive building of any description I'd seen in a long time.

Paragon Referrals, Reception area

As we were in the middle of a nationwide lockdown due to the Coronavirus Pandemic, I followed the instructions I'd received through the mail and phoned reception to let them know I'd arrived with Digby, identified my vehicle, and then took Digby for a little walk around the grounds, allowing him to stretch his legs after our journey, and do whatever he might need to do to relieve himself. We weren't allowed to actually enter the premises. We were only kept waiting a few minutes, when a man I just knew must be Rodney accompanied by a veterinary nurse came out of a side door and walked towards me. I was immediately impressed by Rodney. He was tall and had what I can only describe as a commanding presence. This, I knew, was a man who knew what he was doing, and my confidence rose just from our initial meeting. He introduced himself and his nurse and took a minute to say hello to Digby, who was instantly at ease with him, his tail wagging happily as Rodney fussed and stroked him. Another good sign.

I was given the necessary papers to sign, giving my consent for the operation, and Rodney informed me of just what the day's procedure would entail. He explained that Digby would be anaesthetised after which he would be opened up to allow Rodney to carry out an internal examination of the mass on his spleen. Paragon possesses up to the minute, state of the art facilities so any tests required would be carried out on the mass immediately and the results would be available later that day. Rodney promised to personally call me with Digby's results as soon as he was awake, when he could also give me a time to collect him later that day. As I handed Digby over, I also gave the nurse a lovely new dog sweater we'd bought for Digby. I explained that this was in lieu of a 'buster collar' for after the operation as from long experience we'd found that a dog wearing one of those things becomes something of a target for the other dogs in a pack. Dogs are naturally inquisitive and simply won't leave a dog alone if they're wearing one of those horrible things. The nurse agreed that was a great idea and promised to make sure Digby had his sweater on when I returned to collect him later in the day.

Digby models his new sweater

Digby, (the traitor), happily walked into the building with the nurse, without a backward glance at me. His tail was wagging, and the nurse was talking to him all the way. She was obviously good at her job. I set off for home, but not before phoning Juliet to let her know we'd got there safely, and that Digby was now in professional hands. She couldn't believe it when I told her how he'd happily walked away from me with the nurse, and her reaction was the same as mine.

"The little creep," she laughed.

"Better that way than having to be dragged in and being terrified about what was happening to him," I replied.

"Definitely," Juliet agreed, "I'll let you go, and see you soon.

Oh, how was the journey? Did you find the place easily enough?"

I explained the problems I'd had finding the hospital, and Juliet was more than happy that she hadn't had to try and make the journey instead of me. She won't mind me mentioning that she's a notoriously bad navigator in a car and reading a map would be like trying to read Egyptian hieroglyphics for her. Sorry, darling!

I managed to make my way back to the motorway and was soon happily driving at a decent speed, with the earlier rain having stopped at last. Unfortunately, fate had a nasty twist in store for me that morning. About twenty miles from home, I was cruising at a steady 70 mph, and just about to pass a slower moving truck in the inside lane when I saw something black fall from the rear of the truck. I had little time in which to react. I couldn't risk swerving out of the way into the outside lane of the motorway as that could have caused an accident with traffic going faster than me, so the only thing I could do was carry on and hope the black 'thing' wasn't about to damage my car. I felt and heard an ominous 'bump' from the underside of my vehicle as whatever it was came into contact with my car, but all I could do was hold on to the steering wheel and keep the car going in a straight line. I breathed a sigh of relief as it appeared that no damage had been done, but when I changed from motorway to motorway and slowed down at the roundabout that marked the interchange, I felt a shuddering from under the car and the brakes were making an unusual noise, which plagued me on the rest of the journey home.

I made it home safely and told Juliet what had happened. I had no choice but to go straight to my local garage, explain the problem and hope they could sort it out in time for me to make the return trip to Wakefield later that day.

Thankfully, the two brothers who run the garage are excellent at their jobs and have looked after my cars for over twenty years, so one of them immediately put my car up on the ramp and carried out an examination of the underside. Andy quickly found the problem. Whatever had hit the car had damaged a particular joint on the braking system, (I'm no expert so can't really explain it fully), and as I'd explained that I needed to go back to Wakefield later in the day, he asked me to leave the car with him for a couple of hours and he'd have it fixed for me. Bless him, that meant he would be working through his lunch break, just to help me out so I could go back to collect Digby later in the day. Sure enough, when I returned two hours later, the car was ready and waiting for me and when I asked how much I owed him, he waved me away and said, "Nothing at all, just a simple job." How's that for service?

With a sense of great relief, I drove home and not long after I'd arrived, my mobile phone rang. It was Paragon calling. I answered quickly to hear the voice of Rodney, the oncologist. As he spoke, I began to feel a great sense of relief. He very quickly told me that Digby DID NOT have cancer! Before I grew too complacent, he went on to explain that Digby did however have a very large mass attached to his spleen. Though benign, it would need to be removed, along with his spleen, which was irreparably damaged. The good news was that once the spleen was removed, Digby should have no further problems. Rodney informed me that he'd made an appointment for Digby to be operated on by one of their surgeons, Mickey Tivers, in five days' time. Mickey, who I later discovered is the Head of Surgery, would contact me in the next day or two to speak with me in advance of the operation to tell me exactly how things would proceed. He also told me he would be sending me a photo of the scan that showed the extent of the mass on Digby's spleen. Rodney asked if I had any questions, but I was just so relieved that I couldn't think of a thing to ask, but then Rodney finished by telling me I could collect Digby at 5pm and finished by paying a lovely compliment to our little boy.

"I must say, Digby's a super dog," he said. "He's a real laid-back dude, isn't he? So happy and not a bit of trouble."

I was all smiles as I came away from that phone call and Juliet, who'd heard most of the conversation was smiling from ear to ear. We hugged each other and held one another tightly for a full minute, such was our relief at the good news. Later that afternoon, I set off once again and this time the journey to Wakefield seemed to take less time than the morning's trip, although in reality it was about the same. I was helped by the fact that I'd remembered the correct route to take once I left the motorway and easily found my way to Paragon Referrals, where, after a quick phone call to announce my arrival, Digby was brought out to me, wearing his posh new sweater of course. I was so pleased when I arrived home and Digby positively leaped out of the car, (aided by a little help from me) to get to Juliet who was waiting at the gate for us, after I'd made a quick call to her from the pull-in just after leaving the motorway to say we'd be home in five minutes. She made a big fuss of her little fella of course and in no time, the days flew by until the day of Digby's operation arrived.

Unfortunately, the day of the operation coincided with heavy snowfalls across the country, and it was soon evident that driving to Wakefield in such conditions would be extremely hazardous. Juliet also felt it was too dangerous for me to risk driving in the conditions, so I thought I'd call Paragon to see what the weather conditions were like in Wakefield. Apparently, things were even worse there. The receptionist I spoke to informed me that it was so bad there, that some of the staff, including Mickey the surgeon had been unable to make it into work that morning. Based on that information, she agreed it might be best if I rescheduled Digby's appointment and so we cancelled that day's appointment and Digby's operation was now arranged to take place in three days' time.

In many ways we were very disappointed. After building ourselves up to believe that it would all be over that day, we now had an agonising three more days to wait before Digby could be rid of that horrible mass, growing inside him. It wasn't until later that we discovered just how lucky he was, that we didn't delay much longer.

18

DIGBY'S OPERATION

THE DAY of Digby's rescheduled operation soon arrived and once again me and our boy set off like two intrepid adventurers on yet another trip to Wakefield. Once again, I found my way there without difficulty, (I was getting good at this navigating lark) and after calling to announce our arrival, a nurse came out to the car park to meet us and get me to sign the necessary consent forms. I'd received a phone call from Mickey, the surgeon in the intervening days to say that, depending on how well things went, they would hope to keep Digby in the hospital overnight after his operation and he should be able to come home the following day.

Once again, Digby greeted the nurse with a happy face and a wagging tail and off he went, quite cheerfully as she led him into the building. This time I must have been preoccupied thinking about Digby and the operation because when I arrived at the large roundabout that connected with the motorway, I somehow took the wrong exit and instead of linking up with the M1 (South) that would connect me with the M62, I instead found myself on the M1 (North) heading in the totally wrong direction. Thinking there'd be an exit before long, where I could leave the Northbound motorway and double back to where I'd taken the wrong junction, I drove on, and on, and on. Was I wrong, or what? I drove mile after mile without any sign of an exit, until I eventually saw the signs for a Services area coming up a mile ahead of me. I soon pulled off the motorway and into the Services car park where I turned the engine off and called Juliet to let her know how stupid I'd been. She was surprisingly understanding, and just told me to drive carefully once I got going again. I topped up with fuel while I had the opportunity and was soon mobile once again. I eventually found my way back to the junction I'd originally gone wrong at, and this time found my way onto the correct road and was soon heading in the right direction.

Juliet and I had a good laugh when I eventually found my way home, as she joked that was the kind of thing she could see herself doing, not me, bearing in mind I was once an Area Manager for a large well-known company and my job literally involved me driving all over the country, which I'd done for years without ever having taken a wrong turn, until now!

My morning's road trip was soon forgotten when I received a call from Mickey soon after lunch, informing me that he had completed Digby's operation and that our little boy had just come round from the anaesthetic and was recovering well. He also amused and delighted me by virtually echoing what Rodney had said to me a few days previously, "I have to say, Digby's a super dog, such a laid-back little fella," he said.

Mickey then told me something else that showed how lucky Digby had been. He sent me an email later, that showed exactly what he was referring to when he said that the mass, or abscess as he called it was actually leaking poisonous pus into Digby's body and that, if it had been left even as much as a week longer, it could have proved fatal for him.

Mickey even sent me a colour photograph, taken during the surgery which clearly showed the horrible brown pus leaking out of the abscess. It was truly frightening to think that Digby had literally been just days away from potentially dying from that terrible growth inside his body. I expressed my sincere gratitude to Mickey for what he'd done for Digby, and he promised to call me again in a few days to see how Digby was getting on. I asked if I'd need to bring Digby back to Paragon for his post-op check-up, but Mickey said he'd send all the details to my own vet and that I could book Digby's check up with them instead of having to travel to Wakefield and back once again.

I've reproduced the image taken during the operation, so don't look if you are of a squeamish nature. You can clearly see the horrible brown stuff that was leaking from the mass and potentially poisoning his body.

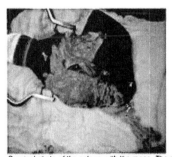

Surgical photo of the spleen with the mass. The mass had been leaking prior to the surgery

He arranged with me that I could call to collect Digby the following morning at around 9.30 am and also said I could phone at any time during the night if I had any worries or concerns. I must say the service from Paragon was fantastic, first class in fact. After the call ended, I waited for Juliet to arrive home, (she was out dog walking when I got the call), so I could give her the good news.

She was so happy when I gave her the good news as soon as she arrived home with Petal and Muffin. I showed her the email with the picture of the mass, and she was thoroughly shocked to see the size of it, and so relieved that Mickey had caught it in time, before the poison had a chance to affect our little boy. All she wanted to do was get hold of Digby and give him lots of love and cuddles, but that would have to wait until the following day. For now, she just shared my relief that everything had gone well, and Digby was going to be okay.

I explained to her that Mickey also told me he would be sending the removed spleen and the mass for further tests, just to be certain there was no cancerous tissue present but he told me he was pretty sure there was very little chance of such an occurrence.

Digby had never spent a night away from home since the day I'd first brought him home over eight years ago, so we hoped he wouldn't be fretting or missing us too much. I tried to reassure Juliet by telling her again just how the staff at Paragon had taken to Digby and how he'd reacted to all the love and cuddles they'd been lavishing on him. We noticed that Muffin and Petal were also quite unsettled when we went to bed that night. Obviously, they'd realised Digby wasn't there in the bedroom and must have been missing him and wondering where he was.

* * *

THAT NIGHT, we both slept fitfully, as we just couldn't wait to bring Digby home. The following day dawned, and we looked out of the window to discover a world blanketed by thick, freezing fog. Just what I didn't need, yet another journey to

Wakefield and back in hazardous driving conditions. Once again, Juliet waved me off with instructions to drive carefully, which I fully intended to comply with. The one thing I hate the most after many years of driving, is fog!

Visibility was greatly reduced as I hit the M18 and headed westward on the first leg of my journey. Even with the car's headlights plus front and rear fog lights switched on I could barely see more than 30 or 40 yards ahead of me, so kept my speed down to a manageable maximum of 50 mph, the most I felt suitable for the conditions. I'd set off a few minutes early to allow for the conditions and was glad to arrive at Paragon in Wakefield no more than around ten minutes behind schedule. I parked as usual, and informed reception of my arrival to collect my boy. While I waited, I phoned Juliet from the car to let her know I'd arrived safely.

Then, as I was about to exit from the car and stretch my legs for five minutes while I waited for Digby to be brought out, what I've since come to think of as the 'curse of the Paragon saga' hit me once again. It's my custom to drive with my driver's side window open by two or three inches, whatever the weather, to maintain a good supply of fresh air in the car while I'm driving. I pressed the switch to close the window and as usual it slid up to the closed position but then, all by itself, it gracefully slid all the way down until it was fully open. I kept trying the switch, but nothing could entice the window to go up to close again.

As my frustration grew, I saw the nurse coming towards me with Digby. I quickly exited from the car and walked to meet them. Digby was so excited to see me, and I knelt down to greet him with a big hug and in return he smothered my face with doggy kisses. After a few seconds of this happy greeting, I stood up and the nurse, with a big smile, gave me the information I required for Digby's immediate post-operative care. She also told me what a good boy he'd been and how everyone had fallen in love with him, and his waggy tail. Seems Digby had charmed the whole staff at Paragon and made himself a little superstar during his time with them.

As it was such a cold morning, I soon had Digby in the car and said goodbye to the nurse, who said I should get a call in a few days to see how he was getting along. Now, my big problem of the day really kicked in. I was going to have to drive home in freezing fog with a dog who'd recently undergone major surgery, in a car with the window locked fully open to the elements. Luckily, I was wearing a warm fleece jacket which would keep me relatively warm but once we got under way, the freezing air soon made itself felt in the car. We hadn't even made it to the motorway and already I was feeling the cold. I turned the collar of my jacket up to try and protect my right side from the worst of the wind chill and pulled over to give me a chance to put my gloves on and at the same time I gave Juliet a ring to tell her we were on our way home, and she couldn't believe it when I told her about the window.

"Is there nothing you can do?" she asked.

"No," I replied. "I've got no choice; I'm going to have to drive in this weather with the window wide open. It's going to be a cold journey home for me and Mr Digby. At least he's got his nice warm sweater on."

Once we hit the motorway, I felt the full force of the freezing conditions and I was just pleased that at least Digby had his sweater on to help keep him warm in the back of the car. I turned the car heater up to maximum as we made our way home and kept talking to Digby as a way of trying to forget how cold I was. Luckily, by the time we left the M18 on the last leg of our journey, the fog was beginning to lift and the sun was breaking through. I rang Juliet and told her to expect us in five minutes. By the time I pulled up outside our house, I was definitely ready for a nice hot coffee but first there was the matter of Digby's homecoming to deal with. Juliet was waiting for us as I got out of the car and lifted the tailgate, gently helping Digby out of the car. He was so pleased to see Juliet, his tail wagging furiously and though he wanted to, I stopped him from jumping up to greet his Mummy. Juliet instead got down to his level, giving him big cuddles as her face was a vision of joy at seeing her special little boy once again.

We quickly went inside the house where the other dogs all waited to say hello to Digby. We carefully allowed them to say their own 'hellos' and I explained Digby's after-care regime to Juliet as she made the most of being reunited with Mr Diggers, while I made myself a hot coffee, just what I needed.

Welcome home, Digby

"What are you going to do about the car?" Juliet asked, in between bouts of hugs and kisses with Digby, who of course, was lapping up the attention.

"Just let me warm up, and then I'll have to nip down to the garage and see if Andy and Shaun can sort it out," I replied. "We certainly can't leave it like that with the window wide open, that's for sure."

"They'll be getting sick of the sight of you," she joked.

"I know, but at least they might make some money on this one," I replied.

The 'greeting ceremony' seemed to go on for ever, as Juliet showed her relief and her happiness at having her Digby back home.

"Did they say anything about the future?" she asked, between cuddles, kisses and lots of tail wagging from our little boy who was obviously so pleased to be home.

"Just that Mickey will ring me in a few days. They're sending the spleen and the mass to their lab to be tested to make sure there's no malignant tissue present, but Mickey says it's just a formality."

Happy to be home!

Considering the fact that he'd undergone such a serious operation, Digby was full of life and showed no sign of being in any pain after the procedure. Mickey had prescribed painkillers and antibiotics for him which he would take until he had his post-op check-up. Juliet removed his sweater for a minute, just to take a look at his operation wound. She looked and was amazed at what she saw.

"There's no stitches," she exclaimed, and I realised I'd forgotten to tell her something.

"Sorry," I responded, apologetically. "I forgot to tell you something about that. Mickey explained to me that there would be no external stitches. They actually glued the wound together. He does have some internal stitches, but they will dissolve and disappear by themselves in a week or two."

Juliet was amazed, as I had been when I learned of the lack of external stitches. From the amount of fur they'd shaved from

Digby, we could see where he'd been glued back together and the operation wound was actually almost the length of his belly! That was one big operation scar.

The other dogs also gathered round, all their tails wagging furiously with happiness, and were all obviously pleased to see Digby, especially his sisters and little Honey. They all insisted on sniffing him, as he obviously carried a very strong 'whiff' of 'vet' and the wonderful thing was, they appeared to sense that Digby was rather fragile and none of them tried to jump on him in excitement or make too much fuss.

Once Digby was settled with his Mum and the other dogs had calmed down, I left them all and took the car down the road to see what could be done about that defective driver's window. More about that in a minute. For now, Digby was home, and everyone was happy, none more so than his mum, who had her special boy home in one piece.

Modern surgery, shaved but no stitches!

19

MUCHAS GRACIAS, CAROLINA

I ARRIVED at my local garage as Juliet happily welcomed Digby home. After my first trip, when I had to get the brakes sorted out, I saw Andy when I went there, who you'll remember was so helpful. This time, I pulled in and was met by his brother Shaun, who smiled in welcome as always and asked what the trouble was. I explained and he took a good look. It was clear to him that the switch for the front drivers' window was faulty and needed replacing, but in the meantime, he said he'd try to do something to get the window raised to keep the car secure from thieves etc.

He spent the next few minutes doing whatever it is mechanics do, and then, as if by magic, with Shaun holding tight to the glass, the window slowly rose until it was in the closed position. Shaun explained to me that the switch needed replacing and that we should refrain from using the window until he could obtain a new one, as if it went down again, we'd have the same problem. Unfortunately, it was likely to take a few weeks to arrive as he would have to order it from Mercedes, in Germany. As both Juliet and I use that window virtually every time we drive the car, we placed brown parcel tape over the switch to remind us not to use it. The brown colour would stand out against the car's colouring and would instantly warn us against using the switch.

Once again, Shaun, as his brother had done just over a week previously, refused to accept any payment for what he'd done in getting the window safely secured for me, saying it was all part of the service. What a wonderful pair these two brothers are. They provide a great service and have done much work for us over the years, but on this, and a couple more occasions, they went out of their way to provide a regular customer with great personal service without charge.

I waited a couple of days and then paid the garage another visit. Shaun greeted me when I got out of the car, and showed great surprise when I forced a small sum of money into his hand and told him it was a thank you gesture from me and Juliet for the help he and Andy had given us. He was genuinely taken aback by my gesture and called to his brother who was in the workshop. When Andy arrived, Shaun showed him the money and told him what it was for. Andy was equally grateful and instead of saying, as I might have expected, that it would buy them a few drinks at the pub, said, "Thanks a lot. This will keep us in coffee for a month. We drink a lot of coffee while we're working."

We've been regular customers of Andy and Shaun for over twenty years, and perhaps you can see just why we'd never dream of going anywhere else for servicing, repairs and anything at all car related. They've cared for every car we've had during that time, Ford, Honda, Peugeot, Citroen and Mercedes. What lovely young men to do business with.

Maybe we should have had a car like this, Diggers

OVER THE NEXT FEW DAYS, Digby continued to get better and better and by now had developed the habit of 'warming the bed' for us every night, much to our amusement. It was quite cute really to arrive in the bedroom to find him on Juliet's pillow, waiting for us to arrive, after which Juliet would make a big fuss of him and give him a cuddle, before ordering him to go to bed. At that point he would happily jump down and cuddle up in his own bed, close to Juliet, and go to sleep. Of course, he also went out of his way to 'milk' his situation and took the

177

opportunity to grab all the extra love and cuddles he could get as he convalesced.

Cuddles with Mum, (Photobombed by Honey)

As he was doing so well, I phoned my vets and made an appointment for Digby to be seen by Carolina in a couple of days, for his post-op check-up. Before the day arrived however, I had a discussion with Juliet, one we'd already touched on during his treatment in Wakefield. We both agreed that not every vet would have gone as far as carrying out a complete examination of a dog while he was under the anaesthetic for his dental surgery. Without any doubt at all, the fact that Carolina had taken that action had led to her discovering the mass on Digby's spleen. In other words, if she hadn't carried out that full examination, we would never have known about the slowly growing and leaking mass inside his body and before long we would have in all probability lost our beautiful Digby.

There was no doubt in our minds that Carolina's professionalism and dedication to her job had actually saved Digby's life! The next day I phoned the veterinary surgery and spoke to a couple of the nurses and receptionists and asked what kind of things Carolina liked. The general consensus was a particular brand of chocolates and so I went shopping and bought a large box of her favourite chocolates, some wrapping paper and a 'Thank You' card.

It's a hard life!

The day of Digby's check-up arrived, and we set off bright and early and arrived in good time for his appointment. I parked the car and rang the surgery to let them know that we were waiting outside, as per the Covid regulations in force at the time which meant owners were not allowed in the surgery with their pets. Carolina soon came out to take Digby in for the check-up, and she asked how he was doing. I told her he was absolutely fine and just itching to get back to going for his daily walks and playtimes. Digby trotted into the surgery beside her, his tail wagging happily. Digby really does like Carolina, who has developed a great relationship with him. As they disappeared into the surgery, I quickly went back to the car and took out the card and present, in a nondescript carrier bag, ready to present to her when she brought him back to me. If she noticed it as she walked Digby out of the surgery a few minutes later, she didn't even mention the bag that had appeared in my hand in the few minutes since she last saw me.

She told me that Digby was doing great, and she was really happy with him. I asked if he could start going for walks again. She said he could go walking from that day but advised us to restrict him to lead walks until Paragon rang to confirm that the tests on the spleen and the abscess gave him the all-clear. From what they'd sent her she saw no reason why there should be any problems.

"Tell me honestly, what the prognosis is for him, from now on," I asked her.

"He should be perfectly normal from now on," she replied. "With the spleen and abscess removed, and no sign of any malignant growth, Digby will be a perfectly happy and healthy dog again."

"I can't get over the fact that he had that thing growing inside him for God knows how long, and he must have felt uncomfortable with it getting bigger and bigger, but he never showed any symptoms of being unwell or in pain."

"As you know, dogs, especially Digby's breed, are very good at masking the signs of illness and any weakness. It's a kind of in-bred self-preservation thing. I'm happy to have been able to help to find it and make sure he got the treatment he needed."

That gave me my opening to pass the bag in my hand to her, saying as I did so, "Carolina, it's not much but this is a little present by way of a thank you from me and Juliet for saving Digby's life. If you hadn't carried out that full examination when he was under the anaesthetic for his dental op, he'd be dead now, because Mickey told me the mass was leaking poison into his body and would have burst within days if they hadn't operated when they did."

I stood back, as Digby sat beside me while Carolina opened the bag and took out the card and present. She smiled a genuine smile of surprise, and I detected a tear of emotion forming at the corner of her eye. I suppose most people just take their vets for granted and rarely think to give them a proper thank you when they perform an outstanding service for their pet. We can be very quick to criticise if things go wrong, and maybe not fast enough to show how much we value them after a situation such as we'd faced with Digby.

"I was just doing my job," she said, "I'm just happy that everything has worked out well for Digby," and he wagged his tail on hearing his name.

"You did more than your job, Carolina. Not every vet would have gone as far as you did to carry out that full examination while he was unconscious. Whatever you might say, we know that Digby owes his life to your care and professionalism, and we'll always be grateful to you."

Despite the Covid regulations, I reached out with my free hand and gave her a very quick one-handed hug of gratitude. I could see she was getting quite emotional, in fact so was I, so I quickly said my goodbyes for the day, and left her to go back to work. I got Digby back into the car, turned the engine on and slowly pulled away, and noticed Carolina was still standing outside the surgery. I put a hand up to wave, and she waved back, still smiling.

A couple of days later, Mickey the surgeon rang me to let

me know Digby had the all-clear. The tests on the spleen and the abscess had proved to be negative for any malignancies. I thanked him again and just to be on the safe side, asked him for a prognosis as I had done with Carolina.

"Digby's clear to return to normal life," he told me, "And, in fact there's another positive way you can look at it. Whatever happens in the future, you can be confident that Digby will never get cancer of the spleen, because he hasn't got one anymore."

I sensed the amusement in his voice, and I laughed.

"That's very true, Mickey. I hadn't thought of it that way."

"You just go and enjoy the rest of Digby's life," he said. "He's a perfectly healthy dog again and should live a full life span from now on."

I thanked him once more and asked him to pass on my thanks to all the staff who'd helped with Digby's care. Juliet was so happy when I gave her the great news. She hugged Digby and made a big fuss of him, especially when I told her that Mickey had also said he could return to a perfectly normal life, including going for his normal walks, on and off-lead, so he would be able to run and play with the other dogs from that day onwards.

It had been a fraught and worrying few weeks and both Juliet and I knew how close we'd come to losing Digby. We'll always be grateful, both to Carolina, the staff at Vets4Pets, and to everyone at Paragon Referrals, who acted so quickly as soon as Carolina referred Digby to them. I just hope Digby appreciates all the work that went into making him the happy, healthy dog he is today.

Waiting for Mum to come home

For the first couple of weeks, we made him wear his sweater when he went out for his walks. We didn't want to risk him getting hurt in the area of his operation by playing too roughly or hurting himself whilst rummaging around in the woods. We were probably being over-protective, but you can never be sure what accidents or traumas lie just around the next corner as we've so markedly discovered with Digby.

Thankfully we were soon back to normal, all the dogs fit and well, and the warm weather making both us and them much happier. As I write this, we're getting ready to celebrate the puppies' ninth birthday, so though it might seem rather weird that we still refer to them as 'the puppies' that's as it's always been and somehow, I don't think we'll be changing that in the future.

Back to normal, Mr Diggers

Of course, for the next few weeks, Digby continued to receive 'special' treatment, and he lapped it up. He carried on jumping on our bed at night. We've never had the heart to stop him. When the dogs are allowed in the lounge in the evening, he tries to make sure he's first in line for cuddles with Mum and when it's treat time, guess who's first in line. None of the other dogs seem to mind taking a back seat where Digby's concerned. It's almost as if they know he had a close call and they're quite happy as long as they have their friend back with them, as playful as ever.

Those few weeks when we thought we might be losing him were some of the most intense times we've been through with our dogs, but of course, Digby is rather special and we're just glad for his sake that everything turned out alright.

All better now!

20

UNTIL WE MEET AGAIN

THOUGH IT WAS ONLY a few short months ago, Digby's illness seems a long time ago to us now. With so many dogs to care for every day we don't have time to dwell on things as they all need our love and attention every day. Thankfully we've had no more crises since Digby's problem and all our dogs are happy and healthy as can be. As the weather has warmed up, they've been spending more time outside in the garden where of course, they have plenty of time and space in which to play and have fun.

Muffin and Petal are definitely pleased to have their brother back 'in the gang' and little Honey is more than happy to carry on being 'the fourth musketeer' in their little gang of playmates. This year has seen the finals of the European Soccer Championships and England missed winning the tournament with a narrow defeat to Italy in the final, losing in a penalty shootout after a 1-1 draw after extra-time. England's penalty taking was simply atrocious. Perhaps they should have picked Muffin for a place in the team. She's brilliant at heading, dribbling, and her nose skills are second to none. Nobody can get that ball away from her. Just look at those dribbling skills!

Muffin, a soccer star of the future?

It seems as if Digby has kind of hogged the limelight somewhat in the second half of this story, but that's purely because he's the one who seems to have been involved in more incidents than the other two in the last year or two.

Muffin is still the joker in the pack of course and she always will be, while Petal is definitely the most serious of the three, who loves nothing better than curling up in the sunshine, or in her bed, and relaxing, in between bouts of frantic play-fighting, romping and rolling around in the garden, and enjoying long walks across the fields and in the woods. Honey, of course, still makes sure she isn't left out of their games and is definitely 'one of the gang' as far as they're concerned.

Little & Large. Muffin with tennis ball while Muffin has the football

Remarkably, we've found that their sense of togetherness is as strong today as it's always been and both Juliet and I love the way they still gather together to pose for photographs. Talk about inseparable.

Posing as usual

There's so much more I could say about our happy little trio, but that would make this book go on for ever, so I'm going to leave it at this point, with our 'one dog with twelve legs' enjoying themselves in the summer sunshine in the garden. When this chapter closes, please stay with me, as I've included a small gallery of some of the photos that didn't necessarily fit in with the narrative and that I hope you'll enjoy perusing.

So, for now, it's not so much 'goodbye' but more 'until we meet again' as I'm sure I'll have more stories to tell you in the future about our wonderful Family of Rescue Dogs.

Sunbathing

GALLERY

The Family of Rescue Dogs Collection

Where's this famous "early bird"?

Petal's ready for Christmas

Peekaboo!

A smile from Sheba to end with

ACKNOWLEDGMENTS

I owe my thanks to quite a few people who had a part in helping me to create the story of Muffin, Digby and Petal. As always, I owe a massive debt of gratitude to my lovely wife, Juliet, not only for her input into the book itself, but for her daily efforts in keeping our family of rescue dogs, fit, fed, exercised and well-groomed. There's no way I could look after all the dogs by myself, and she carries the burden of walking most of them, now that my health prevents me walking them as I used to, restricting me to walking the older, slower and infirm members of the pack, so none of these books could be written without her.

Thanks also to my proof-reader/editor, Debbie Poole who as always has been there to correct any errors I make along the way and suggesting changes where she thinks they're necessary.

To all the staff at Vets 4 Pets in Doncaster, I owe thanks for their continued care, when required, for all our dogs. Their courteous, caring, efficient and professional service has helped to care for our dogs for over twelve years, and my dogs have always been treated like VIPs, (Very Important Pets), from the moment they step through the doors.

In this case I must single out veterinary surgeon, Carolina Montoya Conesa for a very special thank you. If it hadn't been for her diligence, her extra attention to his care during a routine dental operation in finding the mass growing on his spleen, Digby would in all probability have been dead within a couple of weeks. Carolina, your actions saved his life, you were superb, and we love you for being there for Digby when he really needed you.

Likewise, thank you from Juliet, Digby and me to all the staff at Paragon Referrals in Wakefield, especially oncologist Rodney and surgeon Mickey. Between you, you made sure Digby was treated speedily and with great professionalism. Both of you independently told me that Digby was a 'laid back dude' which proved to me that you really care about your canine patients and in the short time they are with you, you form a bond of friendship with them. You were all brilliant, and the fact that Digby is still with us today is a testament to your skills.

Last, but not least I have to say a big thank you to Andy and Shaun Turner at Descars of Doncaster. These two gentlemen definitely 'went the extra mile' in helping to keep me on the road, not once, but twice, during Digby's hospitalisation, as you'll read about later in the book. The service they provided me with, and the speed with which they worked to ensure I was able to make my journeys to the veterinary hospital in Wakefield was absolutely brilliant and they certainly deserve this mention in the book.

Dear reader,
We hope you enjoyed reading *Muffin, Digby and Petal*. Please take a moment to leave a review, even if it's a short one. Your opinion is important to us.

Discover more books by Brian L Porter at https://www.nextchapter.pub/authors/brian-porter-mystery-author-liverpool-united-kingdom

Want to know when one of our books is free or discounted? Join the newsletter at http://eepurl.com/bqqB3H

Best regards,
Brian L Porter and the Next Chapter Team

ABOUT THE AUTHOR

Brian L Porter is an award-winning author, and dog rescuer whose books have also regularly topped the Amazon Best Selling charts, twenty-five of which have to date been Amazon bestsellers. Most recently, his Cold War thriller, *Pestilence*, has been announced as the winner of the Readfree.ly Best Book We've Read all Year Award for 2021. The third book in his Mersey Mystery series, *A Mersey Maiden* was voted The Best Book We've Read All Year, 2018, by the same organisation.

Last Train to Lime Street was voted Top Crime novel in the Top 50 Best Indie Books, 2018. *A Mersey Mariner* was voted the Top Crime Novel in the Top 50 Best Indie Books, 2017 awards, and The Mersey Monastery Murders was also the Top Crime Novel in the Top 50 Best Indie Books, 2019 Awards Meanwhile *Sasha, Sheba: From Hell to Happiness, Cassie's Tale and Remembering Dexter* have all won Best Nonfiction awards. Writing as Brian, he has won a Best Author Award, a Poet of the Year Award, and his thrillers have picked up Best Thriller and Best Mystery Awards.

His short story collection *After Armageddon* is an international bestseller and his moving collection of remembrance poetry, *Lest We Forget*, is also an Amazon best seller.

His children's books, *Alistair the Alligator, Charlie the Caterpillar*, and *Wolf,* written under the Harry Porter name are all Amazon bestsellers.

Last but not least, his collection of romantic poetry, *Of*

Aztecs and Conquistadors, written as Juan Pablo Jalisco is also an international Amazon Bestseller, topping the bestselling rankings in the USA, UK and Canada.

Rescue Dogs are Bestsellers!

In a recent departure from his usual thriller writing, Brian has previously written six bestselling books about the family of rescued dogs who share his home, with this book being the seventh in the series.

Sasha, A Very Special Dog Tale of a Very Special Epi-Dog is now an international #1 bestseller and winner of the Preditors & Editors Best Nonfiction Book, 2016, and was placed 7th in The Best Indie Books of 2016, and *Sheba: From Hell to Happiness* is also now an international #1 bestseller, and award winner as detailed above. Released in 2018, *Cassie's Tale* instantly became the best-selling new release in its category on Amazon in the USA, and subsequently a #1 bestseller in the UK. Most recently the fourth book in the series, *Penny the Railway Pup*, has topped the bestseller charts in the UK and USA. The fifth book in the series, *Remembering Dexter* won the Readfree.ly Best Book of the Year 2019 and has gone on to win another two awards, the first of Brian's books to win more than two literary awards. The sixth book in the series *Dylan the Flying Bedlington* has already won a first nonfiction book award.

If you love dogs, you'll love these seven illustrated offerings with *Muffin, Digby, and Petal, Together Forever* now added to the list.

Many of his books are now available in audio book editions and various translations are available.

Brian lives with his wife, Juliet, and their wonderful pack of nine rescued dogs.

The author

Sasha

Sheba: From Hell to Happiness

Cassie's Tale

Penny the Railway Pup

Remembering Dexter

Dylan the Flying Bedlington

Muffin, Digby and Petal, Together Forever

Short Story Collection

After Armageddon

Remembrance Poetry

Lest We Forget

Children's books as Harry Porter

Wolf

Alistair the Alligator, (Illustrated by Sharon Lewis)

Charlie the Caterpillar (Illustrated by Bonnie Pelton)

As Juan Pablo Jalisco

Of Aztecs and Conquistadors

Many of Brian's books have also been released in translated versions, in Spanish, Italian and Portuguese editions.

Printed in Great Britain
by Amazon

21037257R00130